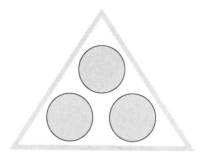

THE SECRET POWER:

*An Empowerment Manual
for Mind, Body, and Spirit*

by Carolyn Boyes

Strategic Book Publishing and Rights Co.

Strategic Book Publishing and Rights Co.
12620 FM 1960, Suite A4-507
Houston, TX 77065
www.sbpra.com

ISBN 978-1-61204-218-3

TABLE OF CONTENTS

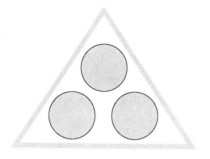

INTRODUCTION

Why can't we have everything? What stops you having good health, finding love, being happy, being successful, and manifesting the sort of life you want? Isn't that what life should really be about?

Is it possible to learn to transform not only your body, but also your mind, emotions and spirit? Is it possible to gain power over your future wellbeing, success, and self-fulfilment?

These sort of questions started bothering me from childhood. I never wanted an ordinary life. I wanted to have an extraordinary life. I wanted to live life as an adventure and discover all the potential that was open to me. But I had no idea where to find out how.

When I was in my early teens, I began to read up on philosophy. I read up on religion. I read about healing and psychic powers. I wanted to know if there was a way in which you could really have it all.

I am not talking about material success, but in terms of fulfilment on every level: what some people would now call total personal empowerment. I knew that the "rules" of life, which the majority of people around me believed in, said this wasn't possible. These rules say that we are not totally in control of what happens in our lives. Yes, we can make a bit of our luck, but we can't fight our genes or fate. What's more, the same people told me again and again that all there was in life was what we could see right in front of us – this world was it. There was no God, no other spirit world, and therefore no power to create your own destiny.

I disagreed. Since then, for over twenty years I have travelled all over the world and investigated different traditions. I discovered a different way of thinking –ways of living going back thousands of years revolving around the idea of a power that doesn't obey the rules we have been brought up to believe in. These different rules say you can have everything, and you can have it any time you want. These rules are known both to Eastern and Western mystery traditions and are gradually becoming better known thanks to books about cosmic ordering and manifestation. According to these rules, you are in control of your destiny. You have the ability within yourself to transform at every level: body, mind, emotions, and spirit.

The Secret Power

The Secret Power is about two kinds of power: the energetic power that the universe is made from, and the power you yourself have as a result of learning to use this energy. The energetic power is the life-giving force of the universe and is sometimes called "the vital force" which underlies all creation, or simply "the force." In the Western traditions, it is called Aether (Ether). In The Secret Power, you will discover how to connect to this energy and use it every day to create the life you want.

Have you ever heard the expression "in the aether/ether?" It refers to something that hasn't quite happened yet, but will soon manifest. Right now, your power is literally in the Aether. *The Secret Power* will show you how to connect to this power to change your future. Aether power is available to you whatever your age, gender or race. It's so simple and easy to use that you can start immediately. Yet knowing this secret is so life changing that you can transform your life in every way. You can change your physical health, you can be happier and you can and create whatever you desire – health, wealth, love, happiness.

Although these may seem big claims to make, they really only begin to tap into the potential of the power you have available to you. Even enlightenment, the goal or every spiritual searcher over thousands of years, can be yours if you use this power consistently and wisely. This is the promise of all the ancient energy traditions on the planet.

What lies ahead?

The power of Aether will change your whole thinking about what you are capable of and what you can make happen in your world. Some people would call this level of empowerment magic and that is not a bad description, though I don't mean showy tricks or the stuff of dark fairy tales in which magicians control others by use of their power.

The magic that is available to you is a loving and powerful force for good and harmony in the world. You can use this magic to heal yourself. You can use this magic to manifest what you want in your life: perhaps you want to live longer, to create a happier life. Perhaps you would like to stay young and healthy, to attract love, bring different circumstances and opportunities into your life, or discover your life's purpose? All these things are possible when you master the power of Aether. You can use this "magic" for spiritual growth, personal development, knowledge, understanding, or even what is sometimes classed as a psychic power – the power to link between people.

If you are like most people in the modern world, you probably only know a fraction of your potential personal power. Most of us use our will power to try to create better lives, and then pray for a miracle when we want more than is on offer or when a crisis happens. When you tap into the energy of the universe, you don't have to pray any more. Instead, through simple techniques from the ancient traditions of the world, you can use the power of Aether consistently in your life to create miracles every day.

How The Secret Power works

In this guide, I will show you a new way of thinking and a set of simple tools that you can use to access the power of Aether so you can change your life every day. I have created a step-by-step body of techniques that are well tested. These tools work. They come from traditions that include three of the oldest spiritual traditions on the planet, from India, China, and Hawaii, and these techniques have been around for thousands of years.

If you use any of these techniques regularly, you will see changes in your life. If you use even one of these techniques consistently, you will create change. If you use all of them, you will notice that your whole life begins to change, as you create change at every level.

Many traditions use energy primarily for physical health. Others primarily promote spiritual growth. My overriding purpose in writing this book is to bring together the teachings so that you can create *complete* health and joy within all of the mind, body, and spirit. None is separate from the other, so by setting out with the intention of building vitality and joy in all parts you will create a stronger whole – magic.

What next?

The Secret Power is divided into three sections:

Part One: *Introducing the Aether Energy System*

Introduces you to the Aether Secret – the ancient knowledge that reveals the power available to you – the invisible power called Aether that underlies the whole universe.

Part Two: *The Four Mastery Methods*

You will learn the four ways to build and master the Aether energy. These methods allow you to awaken, control this energy, and undo any invisible blocks, laying a clear new path for you to create magic in your life. Master this energy and you can create true transformation in your life at any level, mind, body, or spirit, by building your personal power within.

The Four Ways are:

⚠ Mastery of the State – The Breath Method
⚠ Mastery of the Body – Aether Energy Yoga
⚠ Mastery of the Mind – The Mind Method
⚠ Mastery of the Emotions and Spirit – The Spiritual Freedom Method

Part Three: *Creating Magic*

You will learn how to use this power to manifest, heal and even grow your latent psychic powers. You can get clear on what you want to create in your life, and use the power to fulfil your dreams and create a life that is in balance with your purpose and the truth of who you are. You will also learn how energy can be used for self-healing and the healing of others. When you gain this level of ability with energy, this will open you up to gain spiritual under-standing and set you on the path to a purposeful and fulfilled life. You may even choose to experiment and use this power for psychic purposes.

This manual is, however, just a start. I am sure if you have an interest in personal empowerment, you will come across other energy techniques that you can add to your stable. There are many more physical practices that create energetic power, for example. That's fine. I have kept it simple so that once you have mastered these basic tools in *The Secret Power* you can use your power for the health of your mind, body, and spirit. It can promote health and happiness on any or all of these levels. You can then grow your body of techniques and tools as you, I hope, continue to explore the world of energy.

NB: Please, always consult a doctor first about any illness you or another person may have, and never use the Aether healing or other methods as a substitute or replacement for any medical advice or treatment.

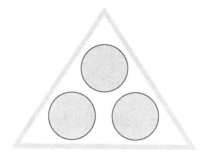

PART ONE

INTRODUCING THE AETHER ENERGY SYSTEM

Why did I grow up thinking I couldn't have everything?

Because I was told there were rules to life.

Here are a few of them:

Anything you can see, hear or feel is real. Anything else is not.

There is no spirit universe.

There is no such thing as magic. Magic is for children.

The body is entirely physical. It is like a machine. If you get an illness, there is nothing you can do. You can't heal without medicine.

Your future is accidental. You can't manifest the future you want.

There are no energetic connections between people. There is no such thing as psychic powers.

This life is all you have got. A lot of your life is just luck: where you are born and the hand you were dealt at birth.

These rules are why so many, perhaps even the majority of people I have met over many years, don't think they can create a future they want other than by working hard or by chance. They think their health is primarily controlled by their genes. They believe that the mind is just part of the machinery of the brain. They don't believe in the existence of any part of the universe that is not visible or cannot be measured. Why? Well, that wouldn't be "real." That would be outside the rules.

In fact, anything other than the "normal" rules would be "magic" and "magic" is just the stuff of fairy tales. Isn't it? Now, "magic" is not a word I use very much, but because our ancestors used to call all this stuff magic then let's give it that label. Can you have everything you want if you don't believe in magic? Well, sadly, I would have to say no. Without magic, you'll always need to settle for limits: limited aspirations, limited happiness, a life limited in potential. Without magic, you'll be living an accidental life, fire-fighting life as you go along.

As it happens, the current majority view that magic isn't possible hasn't always been the case. In fact, legend says that the source of magic has been known about since humankind first walked on the earth. Throughout human history many of our ancestors, even thousands of years ago, completely understood that magic was possible. They also knew that when you gained the power to do magic, the potential for what you could achieve was truly limitless.

Our ancestors understood that to find the source of this magic, and to master it, you needed to somehow move outside your normal five senses – sight, touch, hearing, taste, and smell – and access a universe that exists alongside our normal everyday life. This universe contains one invisible power or energy. Throughout *The Secret Power*, I call this hidden energy, this source of your personal power, and the source of all magic, by its Western name: Aether.

The secret of Aether energy is a very ancient one. While the idea of an invisible power may be new for many of us, thousands of years ago it was taken for granted by our ancestors. They were certain there was a power in the universe that they couldn't see.

Different cultures called this power by different names. In the Greek and hermetic traditions this power is called Aether, the fifth element or Akasha. Scientists call it Ether. In China it is known as Qi (Ch'i), in Japan Ki, in Indian traditions it is Prana. Among Kung Bushmen it is called "Boiling Energy." These names all refer to the same vital energy, although I am sure that some of the names may be more familiar to you than others.

I particularly like the Hawaiian and Polynesian word for this force, Mana, which translates as "The stuff of which magic is made." This power, which for convenience I call Aether, with all its different names and in all its different guises, is the secret stuff of the universe behind every miracle. And once you learn the secrets of the Aether universe and how to access and use it, you can achieve the miracles you want in your life.

In part one of *The Secret Power* you will learn about the basics that allow you to master this energy. You will discover the system that underlies this power behind everything: the power to circumvent the rules and create the future you want and deserve.

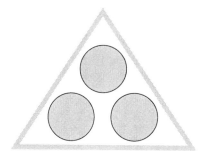

CHAPTER ONE

THE AETHER SECRET

In early civilisations like Egypt, India, and Hawaii, magical knowledge was more widely understood than it is now. Our ancestors understood that this is an energy universe in which there are many forces that are invisible to us. They understood that all life and creative force comes from Aether. Aether is the source of magic: it can be used to manifest events, for psychic purposes, to create a connection with the spirits, for spiritual understanding, even to change the weather or stop a volcanic eruption. All ancient shamans worked with this power.

What is remarkable is that whilst techniques of training students of the power may differ all over the world, at heart the teachings were the same. From Tibet to China to Polynesia, from the Western Hermetic traditions to Eastern Taoism and Tantra, each tradition kept at its foundations the same highly protected secret knowledge that once you understood this power you could do ANYTHING. Using this power would enable you to become the co-creator of your own universe with God. This was the way it was always supposed to be for all of us.

Why was this knowledge a secret?

It is only in the last few decades that this knowledge has started to become more widespread again. So what happened to the original knowledge about Aether power? It is extraordinary that, although it was known to so many cultures around the world, it disappeared. What happened is unclear, but it is said at some point, anywhere between several thousands of years BC and 325 BC, this system of widespread knowledge collapsed, possibly because of abuse of the power. The knowledge went underground and fragmented, and some of the pieces that remained became called this word "magic." The idea of "magic" became an unusual thing rather than something every day. Normal people turned to external gods and idols for rules to live by rather than their inner knowledge, further distancing themselves from the ancient traditions.

Luckily for us, though, some of what is now called magical knowledge was kept safe over the last thousands of years. In the West and the East, in all the great traditions and spiritual centres of the world, small numbers of seekers of knowledge kept the secret hidden away, passed on to those followers who they knew would preserve it. Indeed, the Essene Sect of which Jesus was said to have been a member was apparently one of these traditions.

As the original teachings were hidden away, human beings started to forget the source of power. Academics and scholars began to praise rational, left-brain knowledge and the wisdom of the right, intuitive brain was forgotten. The trouble is the rational mind is all very well, but the mind can block our ability to do magic. So once we learnt to forget to use our intuition in the way our ancestors did, the majority of us lost the means of readily connecting to the power of the Aether energy.

In some countries, bits of magical knowledge survived but over time became lost and fragmented, so there was no longer a complete magical system available for everyone. In the West, in the early days of the Christian Church, some magic was practised, but over hundreds of years this changed and magic was frowned on until the point where practitioners of magic could end up being killed by the authorities by torture, drowning, or execution.

In India the Tantric system, which uses the power of energy, survived, though it too over the years was challenged by newer systems. Other teachings survived in yoga practices in India. The knowledge of energy magic also hung on in various Eastern cultures in different forms, most notably in Tibet as well as in forms of Shamanism, such as Hawaiian and American Indian Shamanism.

A great body of knowledge was kept safe in the Chinese traditions that evolved into the modern martial arts traditions and ways of using the body for health. However, many of the teachings in different parts of the world were under constant pressure of eradication from more "civilised" cultures and teachings.

Why was the knowledge of Aether considered dangerous?

The central idea of mastery of the life force is that man can use his own power to be a co-creator of his own life. Ultimately, giving people back their own power has often been regarded in human history as a very dangerous thing by many authorities, countries, governments and institutions, most notably in later years the established churches, who saw this idea as somehow being in conflict with God, as if mankind was trying to usurp God's power in the universe.

As the centuries rolled on, the idea of a life force or God-given energy became seen as irrational and unscientific. In the West, magic and esoteric knowledge was classed as witchcraft or heresy, and was either considered dangerous to learn or against science.

Over recent years, it is science that has stood against magic. Ironically, the Christian religion considered the knowledge dangerous precisely because it did work, and science considered the knowledge foolish because the assumption was that it didn't work. While the Church assumed historically that magic was powerful but would release the Devil into the world, science assumed that magic is a delusion and smeared it as a superstition. But both the Church and Science share something in common: magic goes against their "truths" and "rules" and so must be stopped.

Back in the Middle Ages, the Christian Church still believed in magic but didn't like the fact that magicians were trying to get powerful results themselves through their will, rather than through the gift of God and through the Church. At this point in its history, the Church certainly believed that these results could be obtained, but that they should come through the Church. If they came about in this manner they were labelled miracles, because they were a gift bestowed from God to the righteous and faithful. On the other hand, magicians didn't try to get the results through the Church and so they were associated with Satan, who went against heaven because he tried to be like God.

The Christian Church was not unique in this attitude to personal power. All over the world, the power of an individual to have power over his or her life was at times not tolerated by religious and other authorities. As the knowledge of energy mastery became hidden, even in the small groups where it was taught it was considered so powerful that in many places it was taught only to a few chosen people who had shown that they were ready to receive and bear the responsibility of this power. Traditionally, in Jewish Kaballah for example, you had to be over 40 to be considered ready enough to be able to take on this knowledge. In the East, qi or prana energy training has long been considered a positive skill to learn when used for health purposes. However, when energy was used for so-called magical purposes this was once again taboo, which is why so many aspects of magical Taoism and Tantra were hidden away.

Despite the fact that so much of the knowledge was hard to find, throughout the centuries many of the wisest and most well known historical figures did indeed practise forms of magic in secret using the power of Aether. These seekers of truth understood that Man was granted free will, and was designed to be co-creator of his universe. They also understood that the magician who works with love does not go against the rules of the universe, but in fact calls on the loving power of the universe for the good of all.

Real energy magic is about recognising man's place in the universe and his unique role in accord with nature. Magic is a tool for using knowledge. The wisest men in most indigenous societies have always been magicians and mystics. They have both wisdom and understanding. They use true magic – a way to cause a change in our world of matter through using the vital energy Aether that links us to the invisible world that is all around us.

True Magic = True Personal Power

Although many magicians use symbols and ritual, and these differ across the world, all use Aether energy. Your ability to create personal power, magic and miracles will come out of your own link with this energy. The awakening of your power has to start with the personal relationship you forge with the life force of the universe.

The reason why so many mystical and magical schools have kept this knowledge hidden over the years is not only one of persecution.

Every individual needs also to be open to understanding their own power and then to spend time clearing their own selves of the blocks they might have – mental, physical or spiritual. Without this understanding and wisdom, the power just won't work. This takes time and consistency, and is the reason why many people never gain personal empowerment.

The Shift and the New Age of Inner Power

Over recent years, perceptions of the way the universe works have begun to change. Some of the resistance and old conditioning is slipping away. There has been a huge Shift throughout the world. This time of a change in human knowledge was predicted many thousands of years ago. It was already known to many ancient peoples that there would be a change in human consciousness, and that the hidden knowledge of the few would now be made available to everyone. Since the end of the last century, this knowledge has been opened up more and more to be shared with the world. The aim of the Shift is to put us in control of more of our own power and for us to understand our real relationship with the universe.

Think how different the world already is compared to only a couple of decades ago. Knowledge is spreading quickly. We already have lives that our ancestors would have thought impossible. We all know more about other cultures and peoples than ever before.

All over the world the once-hidden secrets are being revealed. Wherever you go, East or West, there are esoteric (secret) and magical traditions being taught more openly. Most recently, the secret of cosmic ordering was revealed to a mass audience across the world. More and more people have started to use this knowledge once considered far too dangerous, as it would empower individuals rather than the state and its institutions.

The Opening Up of Hidden Knowledge

One of the great developments in the opening up of once-hidden knowledge to all has come with the immense body of knowledge held by the Chinese. This has emerged as China itself has opened to the world. Suddenly, a wealth of knowledge about energy and its potential has become available to millions of people around the world.

Finally, people are reawakening to the extraordinary abilities they possess. It is now time to unify the knowledge that is held in different parts of the world. The Shift is already impacting you whether you know it or not, by changing our collective link with Aether power. It has already begun to open up the path to *your* inner power.

Unlock your inner power

I think it is very important to end this introduction to the power of Aether by stressing that its power takes habit, but is not complicated to learn in itself. Over thousands of years, seekers of magic have sought to access and control the power and energy known as Aether to create telepathy, clairvoyance and the kind of great strength demonstrated by masters of Martial Arts. However, they believed that gaining mastery over energy was only obtainable through many years of training. In fact, gaining mastery over the secret power can be easy. It is social conditioning which put these barriers up. If you truly desire to know how to master the Aether energy there are simple methods you can learn which will produce extraordinary results. These methods can clear your path to use this power easily every day to change your life.

The most powerful idea within the secret knowledge is that Aether energy can be used purposefully to change the circumstances of your life through the power of thought. What you think and visualise can become real in your future. You may have already experimented with manifesting your future. Has it always worked for you? If it hasn't it is because you have been missing one ingredient – an understanding of the different ways to work with Aether energy.

Indeed, the only way to create consistent and lasting changes in your life is to master the power of Aether at *all* levels of mind, body and spirit.

Now it is your time to be powerful.

In the next parts of *The Secret Power* I will show you methods to access the secret power so you can use this power to change your life and get all the results you want.

You will learn how Aether is the energy that gives you life. It can be stored and circulated in the body, it can be sent via telepathy, it can be used to heal or it can be infused with thought to manifest physical change.

You will also discover how use of Aether power depends on thought – the amount of willpower you, as an individual, can develop to control its force. I will also take you through ways of clearing away personal blocks as well as those that have come from social conditioning – the only limits that prevent you from using this power easily come from your beliefs and the beliefs that you have taken on from others.

Clearing your path to your power may mean changing habits, and also changing your way of thinking. It is because we lack control and awareness that we develop conditions and circum-stances that use energy in habitual ways that don't get us what we want.

But remember, the Aether life force is always ready to respond to new habits. Throughout the centuries people have used the force to produce amazing feats, from physical endurance, to healing, or even producing great wealth or changes in their luck.

Where your mind leads, energy will follow and your life circumstances will change. You can then take *intentional* charge of the power of Aether to enhance every aspect of:

△ your physical life
△ your mental life
△ your emotional life
△ and your spiritual life.

For how, read on. Now is the time that you can uncover this incredible potential that lies in the universe – the energy that is in all life and is the source of life – Aether power. Now you can use the power of Aether to fulfil your dreams every day.

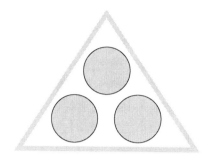

CHAPTER TWO

THE SECRET UNIVERSE

I hold it true that pure thought can grasp reality,
as the ancients dreamed. – Albert Einstein

I believe that if you want to create big changes in your life, you need to rethink the ideas you have about the world. I want you to wipe everything you think you know about life out of your mind and start from the beginning again. Imagine that you have never been told anything about the world you live in, and are now born into this place for the first time. The world you discover is a world that extends beyond the universe of your five senses: the world of spirit and mind as well as of your physical body. This is the universe in which everything is linked by a single energy: the secret power of Aether.

Our ancestors, who understood how to work with energy, didn't have the same view of the world that we do. We tend to think of the universe in a very mechanistic way. However, the universe of energy is a universe that functions not like a machine in which our lives are run according to chance and luck, but a universe that responds to the power of thought and feeling, a universe in which we have control over our lives.

If you can fully take on this way of thinking then everything is open to you. The world becomes a world of infinite potential – a world in which you can create a life of your choosing. As you awaken to your own power by connecting with the Aether energy, you are embarking on a life-transforming journey. You can get rid of all the limits and decide: what is the "everything" you want to have in your life? What is the magic you want? What are the limits you have placed on happiness, health, and fulfilment or understanding in your emotional life, your physical and mental health and in your spiritual life?

YOUR NEW UNIVERSE

If you have never studied any sort of magic, religious or other spiritual practice, you may not fully believe that there is a world beyond the physical, or you may not know how this relates to the way you can control aspects of your life. Many of us in more recent years, especially in the West, are taught that the idea of a spirit universe is the stuff of fantasy or even illusion. The idea that as human beings we can have some part in our futures – what magicians call co-creation – is laughed at by scientists, even though of course science understands that there are many things in the world that exist outside the ability of the normal senses to perceive.

All magicians and spiritual wise men understand that to create what normal people would consider miracles in their lives, you need to get rid of some of the beliefs about the universe you may hold. Our normal senses in the physical world can only detect the dense vibrations of energy, so we generally think of everything we see in our physical universe as being it, and there being nothing else. But the secret hidden teachings of all traditions tell of another part to the universe. At higher vibrations of reality, which are too subtle for our normal senses to detect without training, there is an invisible universe where we exist at the same time as we exist in our physical bodies. This is the home of our spiritual side and also of other bodies that surround our physical bodies, are made up of higher vibrations of Aether, and house our emotions. While we are immediately aware of the physical universe we sense around us, the other is invisible to us much of the time unless you are someone who is born with "second sight" or the ability to connect with other energies.

Let's take a look at some of the operating principles of the whole universe, invisible and visible:

THE UNIVERSE IS VIBRATING

One of the first things to learn about the universe is that it is always in movement.

Let's take more of a look at this. Look around you at the "real" world; what is there? The world we are aware of is physical. It is made up of four elements: earth, air, fire and water. We can see it, smell it, hear it and taste it. If we touch something it seems to be solid. It's real – we can sense it. We can't sense anything else so anything else has to be an illusion – right?

Well – not exactly. Everything we think of as fixed, visible matter is moving or vibrating in a way not visible to us. This is not just a belief belonging to spiritual traditions. Modern science has observed and measured some of this invisible universe, though the universe according to ancient tradition is even more complex than science has yet the ability to measure and observe.

Now, of course we know that there are many things outside the range of our senses. Some sounds are too high to be detected by the human ear. We cannot see particles of matter with the naked eye. Everything we think is solid in the world in fact is vibrating energy. Light travels in waves. Sound travels in waves. Each molecule that makes up what you see through your eyes and sense through your touch as solid is, in fact, vibrating.

The vibrations of Aether

Our ancestors knew long before science got there that some things in the universe vibrate at a slower vibration than others. The slower the vibration the denser the matter; the finer the vibration, the more difficult it is to detect with our five senses. The one most powerful vibration that is outside the awareness of the senses is Aether – the energy and power that makes up the universe. Aether is such a fine vibration that it is invisible to us, yet it is the basic energy of the universe – the finest building block of everything from the stars to every cell of our body.

Aether energy can be described as so small that nothing can be smaller, yet so vast that nothing can be outside it. It can't be felt, seen, smelt, touched or heard. Aether is in every part of nature and every element. Aether flows through the universe in a similar way to water flowing into empty spaces. It is propulsive in nature and sets things in motion.

Aether is the force and energy that makes the whole universe alive – the divine life force that holds the universe together. It allows all the stars and planets and galaxies and different worlds to be in existence. It allows you to be in existence.

Aether itself vibrates at different levels depending on where it is found. At the highest levels you will find the spirit universe. At the denser levels you will find the material universe.

Energy moves through the universe at all times and it moves in patterns, rhythms and cycles. All minerals, plants and creatures that swim and crawl have Aether within them, as does the Earth, along with all other planets. That is why the philosopher Thales said, "all things were full of gods." All things are full of the same energy that is found in the spirit part of the universe where the creating force, known as God, also resides. Imagine, if you will, that God is made of the finest vibration of energy and we are a denser vibration but we are all the same stuff – the stuff of which magic is made, indeed.

We are just a small part of a very big universe. But this universe is not separate from us in any way. It is made of Aether and we are made of Aether, so we are intertwined. In this other universe we can link into other people and parts of nature if we can learn how to connect with its higher vibrations.

Aether, the Life Force

Aether is the energy that flows into our physical bodies and gives us life. The Chinese Taoists said this vital power "fills our whole frames yet man cannot keep track of it… it is dim and dark, showing no outward from, yet in a great stream it flowed into us at our birth." (Guan Zi: Translated by Arthur Whaley)

The story below about Aether comes from the Indian tradition and is a great starting point for understanding invisible energy.

The story goes that one day all the powers of nature that were present in Man were arguing with each other about which of them was the most important and powerful. The breath argued with the ears and the eyes argued with the mind, which argued with the power of speech that argued with the life force Aether.

The arguments went on and on. Finally, to reach a resolution, they agreed that the only way to resolve the matter was to leave the body one by one and see which was most missed.

When the power of speech left, the body was able to carry on without being able to speak. The eyes left and again the body was able to continue, though it was blind. The ears left, leaving the body deaf but alive. The mind left and the body was still able to function, even though it now had no consciousness. The last power to leave the body was the vital power, Aether. Of course, as soon as this began to leave the body, the body began to die. All the other powers rushed to stop Aether leaving.

The moral of this story is evident. The vital energetic power that is Aether controls all of our other faculties. Without energy they cannot function. Think about what happens when a person dies. What is it that gives us life? What is it that departs when someone dies? When someone dies, their body is still there. It still exists in the material world. Yet something isn't the same. We know the person has gone even when their body is still in front of us. The brain waves cease and the person is dead. But what has really departed from the dead person? It is Aether – the vital energy.

You have your own Aether. I have mine. When it is unbalanced or depleted there is sickness. When it leaves the body I am dead. There are many descriptions of the principles of Aether. It is sometimes compared to water, blood or electricity. It is talked about as flowing, rising or sinking. It can be stored, accumulated, depleted or discharged. It is sometimes talked about as being strong or weak, or blocked in its flow.

The Fifth Element

To show how essential Aether is to our existence, Pythagoras called this power the Sacred Fifth Element. The Pythagoreans used the Five-Pointed Star to represent its function. Four of the points of the Five-Pointed Star represent Fire, Earth, Air and Water. The fifth point of the star is Divine Aether, the element without which the others couldn't function. It is also sometimes written in chemistry with the symbol:

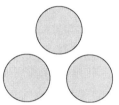

This is a very useful symbol that can be enthused with power through thought, as it can also be used to symbolize the unity of the Three Selves you will learn about in subsequent chapters.

Why Can't I See Aether?

Every part of your physical body is composed of vibrating molecules. You simply translate these vibrations through your senses and give them a meaning so that you think the world is solid. When I look at myself in the mirror I don't see a collection of molecules dancing away, I see a solid shape. When I hear a tune played I turn the different sound waves into the meaning of a melody in my brain.

You can see from this immediately, I'm sure, that although the five senses are useful, they are somewhat limited. They translate all the information they use into meaning which allows us to live our day-to-day lives in the physical world, but they also are not sophisticated enough to sense every detail of what is happening.

Your Connection to the Source and to Nature

The human body is a mirror to nature. Just as the universe flows with the natural waves of spiralling Aether energy, so too does this power flow through not just the physical body, but also the outer layers of the aura, the mind and spirit connecting your whole self to the universe. It is channelled through you directly from the Source, (also known as the Higher "unmanifest" Universe, God, the Dao/Tao, Spirit, or Nature).

Because the basic stuff of Aether energy is the same, everything in life is linked and mirrors everything else. So, for example, your body has energy channels that carry Aether energy through your physical body. You have particularly strong centres of energy in the body known as chakras. The earth too has energy channels, known as ley lines in the West or dragon lines in the East. There are also in different places, particular land formations, or even buildings, which act like condensers for Aether energy.

We respond to the same rhythms as the planets and all of nature without any thinking at all. In magical thinking, we all have times of high energy and times of low energy. There are times of day when it is best to exercise, and times when it is best to be quiet. There are times when our bodies repair themselves, so times when it is best to sleep. This cycle repeats itself again and again.

Because Aether connects us with animals, plants, planets and everything in the world, the health of your mind, body or spirit, and the kind of life you are manifesting for yourself, can all be affected and influenced by the vibrational energy of everything around you. You can be impacted by a location or by the energy of the food you eat, as well as by the people you are with or even by your thoughts and beliefs. Everything you come in contact with carries its own vibration of Aether energy.

How Vibration is Vital to Magic

If you want to create magic in your life you need to expose yourself to the higher vibrations of energy and avoid the lower vibrations of energy. For example, if you are feeling low emotionally, it is a proven fact that being around the beauty of nature will bring your energy up. That is because nature carries higher vibrations of energy than, say, your average office block. You probably know that when you are in a beautiful garden it will have a different effect on you at an emotional, mental, spiritual and even physical level than a concrete city.

One way to think about Aether is to imagine it like a musical note. Lower-note Aether is denser, so found in the material or physical world. Higher-note Aether is found within the spiritual world. But there are many variations of notes within this. Sometimes, you as a human being will be vibrating at a higher frequency than at other times. For example, if you are ill, the Aether in your system will be depleted and your overall frequency will be lowered. If you listen to a beautiful piece of spiritual music or sit in meditation, your vibration will be raised.

Masters of Aether energy have the ability to tune into its different vibrations intentionally, to take advantage of its power. The more in harmony we are with nature, the more restorative it is. This is why sages and hermits will go to a particular place to meditate, for example. They knew that sometimes you needed mountain energy, and sometimes forest energy. They were able to tune in to the different vibrations of energy at very subtle levels and make a decision to go to a particular place to restore mind, body or spirit exactly as needed.

Why some people drain you and others lift your spirits

Teachers of energy have also always understood that the presence of some people may drain you, and others will recharge your batteries. This is according to the vibration of the person you are around. Even though we can't see Aether, we are aware of it through the subtle ways in which we interact with others. This is because the level and types of Aether affect the vibrational frequency of the people. We detect this in the chemistry we have and the feeling we are left with when we interact with a person. The higher the spiritual vibration of a person, the more restorative their presence will be for you. You will notice this immediately with someone who meditates habitually, as they are constantly bringing higher vibrations of Aether into their system.

Someone with strong vital power has a strong influence on others and can be very successful in life. Weak vital power means that you will have little ability to influence your own life or make an impression on others. You have an effect on everyone you interact with depending on the basic vibration of Aether you carry as a person, but also your mood on a particular day. As you impact others, you also impact yourself. A very negative person has a low vibration. A person who is positive is like a magnet, attracting luck and more happiness towards them. I am sure you can think immediately of examples of both types of people around you and the effect they have on you.

If you are someone who brings other people down, just think about the effect you must be having on yourself as well on a daily basis. However, a solution is immediately at hand. When you carry out the exercises in this book, your vibration and general levels of energy will rise. Because, as you will see in the next chapter, your mind, body and spirit are all joined, you cannot impact the health of one without immediately impacting the health of the other two. So improve one part of your life, and the others will follow.

THE THOUGHT UNIVERSE

This brings us to the most important fact about Aether. This is not only a vibrating universe bound together by Aether energy, this is also a universe bound together by thought. Mind is everything.

This is the master key to all energy and magic. The invisible universe contains the source of all creation. Here everything exists in seed form before it exists as a real event or object or person in our physical universe. All Aether energy is infused with thought – it carries thought within it rather like a mirror carries a reflection of whatever looks into it. By connecting with Aether through thought, as you will see in subsequent chapters, you have the power to connect with the source and co-create your physical, mental, emotional or spiritual wellbeing as you intend.

The Law of Attraction

This basic law of the universe is that you attract events, circumstances and people to you based on your vibration. Your vibration is influenced by your thoughts and emotions. If you want to know what your vibration is, look at the people around you for clues. They will reflect in their attitudes and thoughts what is deep inside you.

All the great mystery traditions and shamanic traditions teach us to be aware of how much our thoughts can change our lives. Every thought has its own vibration. This vibration changes everything it comes into contact with, attracting like with like.

Have you ever been into a church or other holy place and noticed how particular the atmosphere is? That's because of all the thoughts that Aether has carried there from all the people who have prayed or meditated there. Generally, these places have a much-raised vibrational energy. Have you ever put on a piece of music and noticed now the room appears changed? Again, that is because the vibration of the words and sounds of the music can change the place they are in.

How your thoughts change your vibration

What you think about changes your vibration as a person.

Positive thoughts give you a positive energy that other people will pick up immediately. Negative thinking repels not only other people, but also positive results in your life.

Thoughts raise or lower your vibration. Because this is a thought universe, all words and thoughts have their own vibration of Aether. If you talk harshly to yourself, even unconsciously, the vibration of your Aether lowered. Thinking positively and speaking positively raises your vibration.

Many spiritual traditions use chanting or mantras in order to raise their vibrational level and connect with the highest vibrations of Aether. If you make a talisman, the intention you put into it will affect the vibration of Aether within the talisman. You can bring in corresponding vibrations of Aether with your original thought vibration.

If you have ever seen a delightful book called The Hidden Messages in Water by Dr Emoto, you will see the effect of words on nature through a startling series of photographs.

Take a look and you will immediately start to change your thoughts about yourself and others if you want to improve your life.

Here is a very quick example: Think right now about being in a peaceful sunny meadow. Straightaway, even thinking about this idea – which is after all just a picture inside your brain – lifts your spirits. This happens because you are tuning in to the vibration of the idea, and the vibration is charged with positive energy.

The world is whatever you think it is. Whatever you think will change your world.

THE POWER OF INTENTION

Everything you think and do affects everything else around you, which is why the law of karma is "do no harm" or it will come back on you. Add to this as well the maxim "think no harm." Everything you do and think will come back to you threefold. If you think good, good will come back. If you think harm, harm will come back. You cannot 'just' observe. Thought travels through the medium of the Aether energy and affects everything the observer observes. Therefore intention is all. Your intention will affect the result of everything you do.

As you will begin to understand when you start to master Aether, whatever you want to change in the universe you can change by thought. What this means is reality really will change depending of the vibration of your thoughts: both conscious and unconscious. The world truly is as you think it is. The world is a creation of the mind. The power of Aether carries the vibration of your thoughts towards the source within the universe and then brings the effect of those thoughts into existence in your reality in the world of matter.

Every thought you think has a consequence. This means that you are creating magic even when you don't realise you are. Everything you think influences you in your real life instantly!

I would urge you, if you want to create change in any level of your life, including your physical body, to start to become aware of your deepest thoughts. Your life exists in its current form entirely because of thought and the vibration of that thought.

Each of us has a different view of what reality is because each of us has different thoughts. If you don't believe that you can have something happen in your life it really won't happen. If you believe that you can find love, get rich, live long, be healthy or whatever it is, you will create it because your thought will act like a magnet and Aether will pull that reality in to your life from the parts of the universe where creation happens.

What kind of life have you created for yourself? What kind of life do you want instead? How can your thoughts support this?

Understand what you need to change and create an intention to bring this about. Even this seemingly simplest of acts will immediately now start to raise your vibration. Aether energy will now help you to start to bring about change.

CYCLES AND RHYTHM

Finally, it is important also to understand how much this is a universe of cycles and rhythm. Think about it. What magic there is in the world! We forget how marvellous this is. Everything around us follows a rhythm, even though we often forget this or take it for granted. The universe rises and falls, expands and contracts. Day becomes night. Night becomes day. The moon waxes and wanes. The sun rises and the sun sets.

Energy governs every part of the universe, so day turns into night, the moon waxes and wanes and the four seasons make up the year. Each year animals are born in the spring, nature emerges from hibernation. In summer nature is in full bloom. As summer dies, trees drop their leaves, plants hide. In winter much of nature hibernates as the energy withdraws.

The months have an energetic cycle that follows the course of the moon. At full moon the energy of nature is at a peak. As the moon wanes, energy sinks, and at the time of the dark moon, nature contracts.

When we use Aether to create change, we do not necessarily see that change manifest immediately because of these cycles. Everything has its time. If you plant a seed, even if you can't see anything happening, it will have its time of fruition. However, it will indeed come into existence unless there is an energetic block. You can learn how to clear these blocks in Part Two.

SUMMARY:

The Physical Universe

The physical or material universe is also known as the "manifest" universe because everything within has a dense vibration. Anything with a dense vibration is picked up by our normal senses.

The physical universe is a universe of time and space.

We have a physical body that lives in the physical world, but we also simultaneously inhabit the invisible universe.

Everything in this universe is composed of the four elements and given life by the fifth: Aether energy.

Every part of the universe operates according to the principles of the Law of Attraction.

The Invisible Universe

The invisible universe is known as the "unmanifest" universe or "the world of spirit" because the frequencies of what lies within it are too high to be observed by us in this physical universe using our normal senses. However, we can learn to tune into this universe by raising our vibration and by using specific energy points of the body, such as the third eye, and the energy point on the crown of the head.

The invisible universe is a universe of a higher frequency vibration than the physical universe. It is composed of the highest vibrations of Aether.

Time has no meaning in the invisible universe.

This universe is such a high vibration, it exists as pure thought or consciousness.

We have bodies (auras) other than our physical body that exist at different frequencies in this universe.

This part of the universe contains the source of all life in the physical universe – the place of creation and the source of consciousness. Life comes about as the result of thought seeded at this level of the universe. Thought travels through the medium of the Aether and creates or "manifests" physical things, people and circumstances in the material universe.

Remember:

The more you learn to master the Aether power, the more you will be able to create *more of what you do want* in your own life *and less of what you don't want*.

I would offer one caveat on this. Make sure, when you are thinking about this even at this early stage, that your intention is right, by which I mean: only ever intend to use any power you gain for the good not just of you, but of everyone in the world. That way you can only do good not harm.

In fact, it is important to say that this is the test of any magical system and any magical teacher. If you don't feel better in your life for learning a way of thinking or using different techniques, stop using them – they are not connecting you with the secret power. If your life feels more balanced and improved, carry on – you are connecting with the power in a harmonious way.

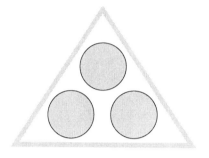

CHAPTER THREE

YOUR PERSONAL POWERHOUSE

Let's take a look at the energetic aetheric "you" in a bit more detail. In this chapter I introduce a useful way to think about yourself from a spiritual way of thinking. From an energetic point of view, you are not just a body with a brain but actually a three-part system. According to different traditions, this is variously described as the body, mind and spirit, or the Three Selves – the Higher Self, the Middle Self and the Lower Self – or the Three Minds: the spirit, conscious mind and unconscious mind. These Three Selves link what we think of as the real or physical universe to the spiritual or invisible universe, and each of your Three Selves has an important role to play in your life. Ultimately, how happy, healthy and fulfilled your life is down to the balance, communication and integration of these Three Selves. This Three-Self System operates like a powerhouse fuelled by Aether energy. It is also is your source of your personal power in all senses of the word.

THE THREE-SELF POWERHOUSE

It is important that you have a clear picture of the operating system of your personal powerhouse in your mind, so here are the basics below.

The Basics

Your body, as has already been said, is just a physical shell. Without Aether it is nothing. What you think of as "you," the self, which is consciousness, is an energetic presence contained in or made up of a series of shadow bodies attached to the physical body.

The physical shadow body mirrors the actual physical body and is the instrument in which both the Lower and Middle Selves live and operate. The shadow of the Middle Self sits within the head region on the physical body. The shadow of the Higher Self sits above the body linked to the Lower Self by a silver energy chord to the crown chakra on top of the head. Each Self has its own vibrational frequency.

These shadow bodies exist on a metaphysical level, and are duplicates of what happens in the physical world. These bodies are also the energy system that holds the physical body together. Everything that exists on a physical level has an aetheric shadow. So, through the Three Selves, we inhabit both universes.

Aka chords

The vital power of Aether is the key that activates the Three-Self System. Aether links the bodies together running through invisible chords and made of an invisible sticky aetheric substance. The Hawaiian shaman tradition has one of the best explanations of this. They call these chords aka chords.

As the Aether travels from one self to another via aka chords it changes vibration. The Lower Self has the lowest vibration. When energy is used by the Middle Self, it is raised to a higher vibration. The Higher Self has the highest voltage of energy. Aka is the perfect carrier of Aether energy. It can stretch and change according to the vibration of the energy within it.

The Higher Self sends us thoughts via Aether. Thought travels through the vital force along the aka chords between the Selves. Your Higher Self, being connected to the source of creation, knows exactly what is best for you in your life, and can create magic for you. It is just waiting to be asked. However, the reason this doesn't happen all the time is because you need a clear channel of communication between your three Selves. Only then can the Aether run through it and bring you what you need to know. We can then start to receive messages from our Higher Self. Messages from your Higher Self, or Spirit, have to travel through the Lower Self or unconscious mind through to your Middle Self or Conscious mind. If you have unconscious mental blocks, then those messages are going to be blocked or come through unclearly.

Thought connections

Thought also travels between us and every other thing on this earth. Every time you think of any part of yourself or any human being on the earth, you send out a sticky aka thread. The stronger the thought, the stronger the thread will be. Eventually, if the threads are strong enough, they become a chord. When you have a chord with another human being, you feel a deep link with the other person even if they are not physically present.

Every thought you think has its own shadow body, and it is linked by aka threads or chords to other thoughts. If you want to undo old thinking patterns that hold you back in your life, you can do this by changing the energetic patterns of the thought and thus undoing the chords.

The Three-Self System

The Middle Self – Also known as the Conscious Mind

The Self you are probably most aware of is your Middle Self, or conscious mind. It is the one you are thinking with as you are reading right now. It is rational and logical and has imagination. It is also the only part of us that can sin, because you can create bad intention to do bad magic as well as good. Your conscience or Higher Self will let you know when you are doing this, to stop you eventually bringing bad karma into your life as a result of your thoughts and actions.

Your conscious mind is sometimes referred to as the monkey mind because it thinks it is in charge and all-powerful, when in fact it is little without the other two minds. The Aether vibration within the Middle Self is fuelled by your thoughts, your beliefs, your breath and the vibration of the food you take in. Your Middle Self is linked by aka chords directly to the unconscious mind but not to the Higher Self. Thoughts that travel along the Aether to the Lower Self are stored by the Lower Self as attachments or thought forms that can be detected in the aura. These can block Aether flow to the Higher Self and your spiritual connection.

SUMMARY:

The Conscious Mind/ Middle Self

The conscious mind is designed to be logical, reasoning and rational, but also has a conscience so knows right from wrong.

It has free will, however, so is the only Self that can sin and cause pain or harm to another, including to its own Lower Self.

It can also give instructions to the Lower Self rather like the captain on a ship gives instructions to his crew. It makes decisions on a day-by-day basis based on conscience and logic.

It has no direct aka connection to the Spirit or Higher Self but has to communicate via the medium of the Lower Self.

The Lower Self, also known as the Unconscious Mind

There is also another Self you may sometimes be aware of: your subconscious, unconscious mind, or Lower Self. On a day-to-day basis your conscious mind seems to be in charge, but it has a minute part of the power of your unconscious mind. Your unconscious mind is busy all the time you are not thinking about it, which is why, of course, it is unconscious.

For example, until I suggested it as you are reading this now, were you aware of the feeling of your right arm, or your left leg? If you weren't, that is because they were outside your conscious awareness but inside the remit of the unconscious mind. While our conscious minds notice about seven bits of information per second, our unconscious minds are taking in at least a million more bits of information about the world. The unconscious observes and stores all this information and then processes it according to our beliefs to construct our reality in cooperation with the Higher Self or Spirit.

The Lower Self inhabits a shadow body around and within the physical body. It is the intelligence within the physical body, controlling our physical survival through the functions of our vital organs that are necessary for us to stay alive. Your unconscious has the potential for a perfect blueprint of what a perfectly functioning body should be like. If something goes wrong with our physical bodies, something has also gone awry at the unconscious level.

Your Attachments and Negative Emotions

This unconscious part is like a black bag containing all the fears and desires, guilt and attachments that control our focus in life. If there are few attachments or negative emotions and beliefs in the unconsciousness, then the Aether energy flows easily through to the other two selves. If we have many thought attachments then people who can sense higher levels of energy can sense these attachments as thought forms or shapes or feelings within the other bodies.

Vital force that enters the body from the air and food is stored by the Lower Self within the energy centres of the shadow body. It can be used by the middle self as willpower. Energy is raised from the energy centres of the shadow body of the Lower Self to the shadow body of the Middle Self around the head area.

The quality of Aether flowing between the Lower and Middle Selves governs how positive your mental energy is and how enthusiastic you are. It can be blocked by toxic beliefs and negative emotions. Attachments or negative thought forms in the Aether can lead to addictions and other types of craving or harmful desires, as well as false fears, depression and stress. Balanced Aether brings balance in the mind and a feeling of contentment with life, as well as a feeling of freedom and independence. When it is unbalanced, we tend to cling to false ideas and idols and we act with pride, arrogance or weakness in our relationships with others. At the most extreme, attachments and blocks can cause mental instability and derangement.

Two prime functions of the unconscious are to create memory and to run the body. If we didn't have a memory, we would never be able to learn anything; we would have no sense of identity. In the magical way of thinking, the unconscious mind stores both genetic memory and personal or learned memory. The important thing about memory is that it doesn't exist just within the physical brain; it is stored as a vibration or frequency within the cells of the body.

Often, Aether energy can get stuck within the body – for example, through a build-up of negative emotions or thought patterns. Think about a negative memory right now, and you will notice that just thinking about it creates tension in your body. Imagine what would happen to your body if you continued to think negative thought after negative thought. The memories would cause blocks within your Aether that may result in physical or mental problems. However, if you create positive thoughts and memories in your mind, you will create positive movements of Aether around your body. You will learn later in the book how to intention undo vibrational Aether blocks within the body, and you will be able to release physical, mental and even spiritual healing in the body.

If you want to create a good rapport with your unconscious Lower Self, you need to treat it in loving way. You can think of the Lower Self as a child. You need to be kind to it but at the same time be firm and disciplined in the way you talk to it, giving it clear instructions. The Middle Self is like a rational parent to the child of the Lower Self. The Higher Self is like a loving parent to the Middle Self. Each self is a different level of consciousness. Set up the relationship correctly and the relationship will work well. If not, there will be some imbalance in some part of your life.

SUMMARY:
The Unconscious Mind/ Lower Self

The Lower Self looks after our memories, storing and organising them, including repressing those that are unresolved and would release negative emotions that you are not ready to cope with.

It also is a storehouse of your emotions: repressing unresolved emotions for your protection. When it believes you are ready emotionally and spiritually, it releases repressed emotions so that you can rationalise them and release them from the shadow body.

It controls the moment-by-moment running of every cell of the body. It contains a blueprint of the perfect physical body that is why it knows how to heal and restore what has been damaged.

Despite its resources it follows the orders of the Middle Self (conscious mind) as long as there is a clear energetic channel between the two. However, it does not follow the orders of the conscious mind if there is no trust between the two. Trust is destroyed when the conscious mind has got into the habit of ignoring messages from the unconscious.

The Lower Self hears all thoughts as instructions about what to manifest in your life on a physical level. This includes the negative comments we make to ourselves. So, if you beat yourself up, the unconscious will hear you and behave according to this self-belief. To get a good rapport with your unconscious, learn to make clear pictures of the life you want to build in your mind's eye.

The Lower Self accumulates and circulates Aether energy around the body. Energy can be generated and increased or decreased either through physical exercise or direct instructions from the Middle Self.

It is a highly moral being doing only what it believes is to your highest good.

It provides the link to the Higher Self for the conscious mind. We can only have a spiritual or mystical experience if we have a clear channel through the unconscious mind.

It talks in symbols and pictures. The unconscious will throw up symbols (as the psychologist Carl Jung understood), as a way of telling us what we need to know about everything from our health to our life purpose. This is why it is important to listen to your dreams and meditations.

It likes habit and consistency. Build new habits of thought and energy raising and the unconscious will reward you – with good health and positive emotions.

It is able to use telepathy and clairvoyance because it links to the Higher Self.

It occupies the shadow of the physical body and looks like the physical body, but in energetic form.

The Higher Self

From time to time, perhaps you have felt linked to another aspect of yourself. When have you had a spiritual, magical or mystical experience? This is when you have felt the presence of your third self or Higher Self, which is also sometimes called the Spirit, Cosmic Self, Super Conscious or your Guardian Angel. Your Higher Self is itself a form of consciousness energy. In Hawaii it is called kahane, a word that means "the creator of the universe." The name is used because you are co-creator of the universe though the medium of the Higher Self. It is your true unlimited powerful self, which is linked directly to the great limitless consciousness that forms the invisible universe and contains the source of all.

The Higher Self also inhabits a spiritual shadow body. This is also made of Aether energy, but of a higher vibration than your other bodies. It connects with the highest levels and powers within the energetic universe, as well as the Higher Self of every creature on the planet.

One of the key purposes of the Higher Self is to construct your future. It intuitively knows what is fixed and what it is possible to change; it also can see all of your past and present. It constructs your future based on the conscious and unconscious thoughts coming through from the middle and low selves. In effect, the Higher Self averages all these thoughts to materialize real events in your future. If the thoughts in the middle and low selves change, your future will also change. So if you want to manifest a different life in any way, you need to change your life first on a thought level.

SUMMARY:

The Higher Self

The Higher Self is a perfectly balanced parent and guardian, sometimes referred to as your Guardian Angel – a balance of female and male Aether energy. It is your individual expression of God – a perfect expression of who you are.

It is your personal link with God, and it links to every other Higher Self in the universe and to all of nature. This is the Self through which you feel a sense of oneness with others, nature and God.

It both knows and can affect the future. It knows the source of everything happening in your life at this moment. It sits above time and space and sees all, including past lives. If you want to know your future, you can know this if you connect through the unconscious to the Higher Self.

To form your own future through cosmic ordering, you must communicate with the Higher Self, again through the medium of the Lower Self.

It cannot make mistakes. It is totally trustworthy, loving and filled with compassion.

It cannot interfere with your free will, but it can clear false attachments and energetic blocks from the Lower Self that will help you to come nearer to your life purpose.

The Higher Self will send you messages via your dreams. It also gives you intuitions. These are designed again to help you stay on track with your life and avoid unnecessary pain and suffering.

The Source of Creation

The Three-Self System creates your life, past present and future, on a moment-by-moment basis. The way you do this is through the flow of energy carrying thought between your Middle, Lower and Higher Selves. Because the universe we live in is composed of pure consciousness, every thought we have, conscious or unconscious, affects what happens in the now. Every circumstance and event that happens to us, including our destiny and health, comes from the seed sown in the invisible universe before it happens in our material world.

Many traditions have ways of using this power with intention. This is the core of the Aether Secret Method. If we harmonize our higher and lower selves with our middle self, we can intentionally make miracles occur in our lives on ANY LEVEL.

AETHER WITHIN YOUR POWERHOUSE SYSTEM

The type or vibration frequency of the Aether within your Three-Self System varies, but it is essentially the same energy. In order to do magic, you need to learn to connect with the highest frequencies of Aether.

High-Voltage or Universal Aether

The highest vibration frequencies of Aether are found in the universal Aether energy, sometimes called Akasha or mana loa – the supreme force. It is luminous energy made up of pure love, and infinite. It is of the highest vibration or voltage. This Aether is pure Spirit, and found at the most subtle levels of the universe.

Universal Aether is the source of all life. It is an infinite source of energy that we can call on if we know how, to restore balance to the mind and spirit as well as to the body. This high-voltage Aether is the pure consciousness energy existing on a cosmic level. At this level of the universe, we are no longer individuals but we link in with other Higher Selves, including the souls of those people who are no longer on the earth plane.

This vibration of Aether functions as the force of creation. Aether is the master creative power in the universe. We owe our existence in the material world to this power. Pure Aether is the original creative power that made the universe. It is literally vital, not only because it gives us life, but because it gives everything in the universe life. By linking in with this level of Aether you can bring life to thought and turn your desires into "reality," or what has become known as cosmic ordering. You can also link to every other part of nature in existence from other human souls to nature on the earth and to other vibrations. This form of Aether is of a much more subtle vibration than that found in the body, but can nevertheless be used for health and healing within either the physical body or the mind. When we are deficient in our own energy, we can draw on the extra universal Aether. As long as the Three-Self System is free of blocks, empty and calm, the vital Aether energy can find its way through to where it is needed.

Middle-Voltage Aether

The middle voltage or frequency of Aether is sometimes called double Aether, mana mana, or the astral light. It has double the power of the Aether within the Lower Self or shadow body around and within the physical body. This demonstrates that you can have sway over your physical body, something you will learn to do within the Aether methods in Part Two.

Low-Voltage Aether

The lower voltages or vibrations of Aether are sometimes called qi, ether or mana. We each have an amount of vital power within us at birth, which can vary. This is known as your original Aether. This lower-voltage original Aether is inherited by us from Spirit. When you are born, your physical body is the sheath through which the Aether flows and gives you life. If there were no Aether energy, the physical body would simply be like a lump of unformed clay.

At the highest part of spirit there is one source, God, but it has two aspects to it: male and female. These aspects are our cosmic parents (meaning the Aether within the lower Self is perfectly balanced with yin and yang, or male and female, energy). The amount and vibrational quality of Aether in your physical and aetheric bodies will influence your emotional and physical health. The Aether in your physical body is still the same basic energy as the Aether found in the higher vibrations of the universe, but in order to give life within this material universe, it has to become of a lower vibration, because it needs to penetrate the dense molecular matter of the physical body.

You can boost the vibration of the Aether in your body through the regular practice of Aether Yoga (see Part Two), which balances both the male and female aspect of your Aether energy.

SUMMARY:

Always bear in mind that you are a treasure house of infinite power made up not just of one "Self" but of three "Selves": mind, body and spirit, filled with and fuelled by Aether. When these three selves are in harmony the amount of Aether power available to you is infinite.

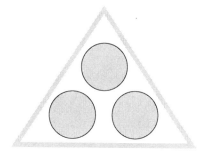

CHAPTER FOUR

THE ENERGETIC BODY
AND HEALTH

*The energy by which the body is pervaded is the same as that
which illuminates the world and maintains alive all beings.*
—Joseph Campbell

Let's take a deeper look now at the energy systems of the body.
This will help you to understand how energy circulates in the body,
so that you can learn to sense energy movements in your body and,
from this, begin to connect with the different vibrations of the
energy in your whole Three-Self System. It will also help you if you
want to use Aether power for healing through the methods you will
learn in Part Three.

The Energetic Body

The understanding of energy within the body comes from some

of the oldest traditions on the planet. It has been documented since at least 4700 years ago, the time of the Yellow Emperor in China, and is believed to have been known at a similar time in places like India and Tibet. However, it probably goes back even further in time than this.

Ancient traditions say that when we are born, we are like a piece of unmolded clay. Without energy, we are without life. Energy pours into our bodies through the energetic connections we have to the universe. We are born with energy filled with genetic memory from our parents. Your physical body is made up of two parts. The first part is the physical body. The second part is the invisible shadow body around the body, in which the unconscious lives, and which is composed of energy. The shadow around the body is often seen as light. It extends beyond the physical body by about four or five inches. It is also within your physical body, which means that every cell of your body contains Aether.

Aether moulds the body flowing through various energetic channels, known as meridians. As it flows through, it is able to mould the organs, features, tissues and cells of the body according to a perfect spiritual blueprint. Low-voltage Aether flows through energetic openings in the body, which are in the head, ears, eyes, mouth and nostrils, and opens up each part of the body in turn.

Your Health and Original Aether

How much vital energy you have and the quality of the vital energy you have determine your health. Over time, your gift of original Aether becomes depleted unless one of two things happens: either the amount of original Aether is preserved to prevent depletion of the life energy, or extra universal energy is called on to refresh the body.

Health in the physical body can be boosted by the right kind of exercise and nutrition. However, the opposite is also true. If you neglect your mind, body or spirit and live out of rhythm with your environment, you cause imbalance in the whole of your system. Imbalances in energy flow can be caused by physical factors such as poor nutrition, too much or too little sexual activity, and too much work or exercise.

Health also depends on your thoughts, emotions and behaviour, as well as your genetic memory and nutrition. It is important to think that the human body does not operate in a vacuum. Your physical, mental and spiritual energy and health can also be influenced by the external environment: where we are, the temperature, and even colours, tastes and smells. In other words, we are all just parts of a bigger whole.

SUMMARY:

Vital energy affects your health in the body.

It affects your mental health and influences it.

It affects your spiritual health.

Anything you do or think can cause an imbalance or heal on each level: physical, mental and spiritual.

The Seven Emotions

You are designed to have emotions, and in general, emotions ebb and flow and do not harm the health of your Three-Self System. However, if you have sudden extremes, or emotion over a long time, it can result in disease in the body, because it causes an imbalance in the energy body.

There are seven kinds of emotion, according to Chinese energy thinking. These include happiness, anger, sadness, anxiety, grief, horror, and fear. Too much negative emotion has an effect on particular organs of the body. Anger hurts the liver, anxiety depletes the spleen, sadness hurts the lungs and fear depletes the kidneys. Even too much joy or happiness in Chinese thinking can be negative by the way as it can turn to hysteria.

What affects the shadow body will affect the physical body and vice versa. Because the unconscious Lower Self is in charge of both emotions and the physical organs and cells of the body, emotional distress can either affect the physical body immediately or manifest after years within the cells of the body, for example, as a serious disease like cancer. Also, because the Lower Self links directly to the Middle Self, which is the seat of mental activity, mental strain and stress can show up in physical ill health. We lose energy when we spend too much time worrying about external life. Likewise, because the Lower Self links directly to your Higher spiritual Self, spiritual disturbances will also be registered within the physical body.

For health in the body we need to have our vital energy flowing properly and an adequate supply. Stagnant energy in the body, mind or spirit breads disease in these areas. It becomes rather like a stagnant pool of water. If light is not shone on it and the flow restored to the pool, it breeds disease. When the energy system is working well in the body, it forms a basis for us to work with the subtler energies of Universal Aether and produce greater effects in our lives. This has been described as being in the way that steam rises from water boiling in a pan.

Ensuring a strong flow of energy means that disease does not develop in the body. The supply of energy in the body can be depleted. It is rather like a rechargeable battery that is either full or running out of power. If it starts to run out of power and we don't know how to recharge it, we start to lose functions in the body. Its function in the body is in some ways like blood, in that it brings nutrients to all parts of the body for the body to function; however, in this case it is life itself that comes into the body. When it is flowing well, every cell of the body is full of life. Moreover, possible starting points of disease are removed just like the blood carries away waste.

The purpose of many Eastern practices such as Qigong, yoga and Tai ch'i is to make sure that the body-mind system stays strong by ensuring that any blocks to the flow of Aether through the system are removed, making the best use of available vital power.

THE ENERGY CHANNELS
The meridians –main energy channels of the body

The main energy channels of the body are called meridians. These are the means through which energy flows from the universal source into the empty husk of the body, making it alive at birth. The energy that comes into the physical body is a heavier vibration than the energy of the spirit universe, but still has life-giving qualities. Throughout our lives, the flow of energy through the meridians determines the quality of your health.

Aether energy is in every cell and part of the body. There is no part of the body that does not contain this force. Energy goes out of the body and gives rise to the aura. Disturbances in the aura indicate disease in the body. Protective energy forms a barrier around the body. It flows under the skin from the meridians. It allows healing energy in and keeps harmful energy out when it is working properly. It controls the temperature of the body, and functions like sweating.

The primary energy channel: The caduceus

The primary energy channel of the body connects the perineum with the crown and contains the seven energy vortexes, or chakras, as they are known most generally. It is called the shushumna in India. In the Western Hermetic tradition it is the caduceus, the symbol you will often seen used for the medical profession, which is also used as a symbol in Western Magik.

There is a meridian down the midline of the body, and then the superconductor of the body is the channel that runs along the spine. The spine is known to be an important route for energy in most systems, which is why most meditations encourage a straight back, so energy can flow into the body through the universal source.

If the energy in the meridians becomes blocked, imbalanced or stagnates, the effect of this on the body is disease. You can stimulate or sedate the passage of energy through the meridians through massage, tapping, and practices such as acupuncture and heat. In addition, you can accumulate more Aether energy in the body through deliberate mind practices such as the Aether Mind method.

The energy numbers: 12, 365 and 7

In total, there are twelve major meridians within the body (the easy way to remember this is it's the same as the number as the months of the year), which correspond to the twelve organs of the body.

In addition there are 365 acupuncture points (the same number as the days of the year), which are points that can be used to influence the flow of energy through the body.

There are seven major chakras or energy clusters on the body (the same number as the days of the week).

Accumulating Aether

You are an energy system. The amount of energy in the system depends not just on good flow of energy, but also on accumulating energy. You have three key points for energy in your body, according to the Chinese way of energy, corresponding to three of the chakras. These are located at your third eye (the point between the eyebrows) and just below your navel and at the heart; in other words, a central point for each of the lower and upper points of the body and head. You can think of these energy centres of the body as places where Aether is charged or stored. It is as if they act as rechargeable batteries for the body.

Your ideal in mastering Aether energy is to harmonise the mind, body and spirit by opening and clearing the channels between the three selves. Clearing the physical channels in the body and ensuring strong energy at each of the key energy points of the body will set the foundations for this.

The Seven Chakras

The seven major chakras are centres of spiralling energy which are three to four inches across. Imagine them like the power stations of the body. Each chakra, when it is functioning properly, pumps life energy through the physical body. If the energy is depleted, the vital organs of the body will become diseased or ill.

You can visualise these points in meditation work as flowers with their petals open or as wheels of swirling energy. Intending the energy centres of the body are kept clear while meditating tells the lower self to restore the health and right functioning of the chakras. You may also sense energy gathering in these centres as you become more sensitized to Aether and also feel the subtle differences in vibrations between the chakras. Energy Yoga will help you to charge and accumulate energy within the third eye and base.

Seven: Crown Chakra

The crown chakra is your direct link to the higher energies and your higher self, so is the chakra of pure consciousness. It is located at the crown of the head, at the middle, between the left and right ears. It controls the pineal gland and the brain, and flows energy

through the spine to the entire body. In Chinese this point is called
the Ba Hui point, and is the master point of the meridians. It
literally means "the point where all the rivers meet." In India this
is the Sahasrara, and is symbolized by a lotus with one thousand
petals. This point being in balance calms the brain, clears the sense
organs and expels stress from the body and mind.

Six: The Third Eye

The third eye sits between the eyebrows, and is the seat of the
energy of consciousness. It is also sometimes called the ajna chakra
or the master chakra. It controls the pituitary gland and the
endocrine glands. It is responsible for storing energy that can be
used for spiritual connections and is your psychic connection, as
we will see in later chapters, as well as your gate to intuition. In
Chinese energy systems it is known as the Shang Dan Tian, or upper
Dan Tian in the Chinese system.

Five: Throat Chakra

The throat chakra or vishuddhi is at the centre of the throat and
controls the voice, thyroid glands, parathyroid glands, and
lymphatic system. It governs self-expression and communication as
well as clear thought.

Four: Heart Chakra

The heart, the Middle Dan Tian or anahata, is an important
energy centre across most areas. There is a front heart chakra,
generally thought of as the heart chakra, and also a back heart
chakra. The front chakra controls the physical heart as well as the
circulatory system. The back chakra controls the lungs and the
thymus gland. Emotionally, it governs your capacity for unconditional love.

Three: Solar Plexus

The solar plexus is the lower Dan Tian or manipura, the key point of the body for accumulating energy. On a physical level it governs the health of your digestion. On a mental level it is your personal power point. If it is damaged you may have fears, anxieties or extreme introversion. This is also, of course, your gut instinct point.

Two: Sacral Chakra

This is the reproductive energy centre and also the centre for joy and enthusiasm and basic emotional needs. It is known as swadhisthana in the Indian system. If out of balance it can give rise to addictions and damaged relationships.

One: Base

The base chakra located at the perineum below the genitals and by the base of the coccyx. It is known as muladhara in the Indian system. The base chakra sends energy throughout the physical body, and particularly affects the spine and sexual organs. It also contributes to a feeling of being grounded. This is responsible for storing "essence" or sexual related Aether energy. It is our survival and security centre.

The Dan Tian – the "fountain which never dries"

Key to the accumulation of energy in the body is what the Chinese call the Dan Tian (called the hara by practitioners of Japanese martial arts, and the key qi (ch'i) point of the body). The Dan Tian stores Aether energy and pumps it where needed to the organs and cells of the body. The word dan is a Chinese word meaning elixir, and the word tian in Chinese means field. Eastern energy practices aim to accumulate energy or "essence" in the Dan Tian and then harvest this energy and flow it around the body for physical health and healing. If the Dan Tian is in good shape then the foundations of the body are strong.

Another Chinese name for this Dan Tian is qi hai, or the 'sea of energy'. Many disciplines, including Zen meditation and martial arts, stress the importance of placing one's mind into the Dan Tian. If you bring your attention down to this point it brings your mind down into your body, balancing your thoughts at the same time it strengthens your body.

If you want to test this on a very basic level, try the old Aikido trick. Stand up straight and ask someone to lift you up. Unless you are particularly heavy they will probably be able to do this quite easily. However, try this again. This time concentrate on bringing all your energy down into your Dan Tian. You will find it is much more difficult for the other person to lift you up, as the Dan Tian acts as a core gravity centre for the body. Focus on building this core through mental focus and accumulating energy through yoga. When you function from your Dan Tian on a daily basis you will come across to others as someone with gravitas, mastery of self and a person who is balanced and harmonious but "with guts." Accumulating energy in the Dan Tian can help everything from back pain to alleviating depression.

NEXT STEPS

To gain mastery over Aether energy either for healing or manifestation, you need to pay attention to all our bodies, physical, mental, emotional and spiritual. By looking after the health of your energetic body you nurture your energy. In the next chapter you will see how to connect with Aether energy. Then, in part three of *The Secret Power*, you will learn how to heal the body using the energetic system.

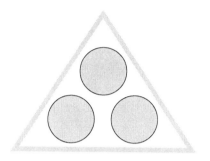

PART TWO

INTRODUCING THE FOUR MASTERY METHODS

When your mind is clear, your body is clear.
When your body is clear, your energy is clear
When your energy is clear, your mind is clear.
When all is clear, your spirit is free to fly.

— Anonymous

In the next four chapters, you will learn the FOUR Mastery methods – ways to perfectly harmonize your Three-Self System (mind, body and spirit/ Higher, Middle and Lower Selves) and to master the different vibrations of Aether energy for personal empowerment.

Connecting with Energy

You can train yourself to preserve and accumulate Aether energy by using regular physical practices as well as mental and spiritual practices. These ensure that you stay healthy physically as well as mentally, and harmonise the connections between each of the Three Selves.

The Aether that keeps you healthy can be kept strong and vital through physical exercises like Aether Yoga, which opens up the energy channels of the body. You can direct the energy to different parts of your body, and direct energy outside your body. Aether flow can also be boosted through the Mind and the Spiritual Freedom Methods, which release emotional, mental and physical blocks within the unconscious, deliberately infusing the Aether with positive loving thoughts. If you deplete the energy you are born with in your body, you can renew the energy by drawing on extra energy from the universal source through altering your state through your breathing.

THE FOUR METHODS

The Four Mastery Methods are ways to "Clear Your Path", a term that means "to make you free you from energetic blocks in the channels between the selves." In doing this you raise your sensitivity to Aether Energy. This allows you to begin your journey of mastery over the energy in its various vibrations at a physical, mental and spiritual level. You can then use the Aether Secret into your own life to create health, wealth and happiness, as well as extrasensory powers.

The mastery methods are very simple habits you can adopt immediately. Yet, although they are simple, you will find they create profound change in your life.

First, you learn to free up your flow of life energy, then you will find every part of your life flows more freely.

To be healthy in mind, body and spirit you need to have a balance of energy, neither too much nor too little. To have a happy, healthy life you need to pay attention to mind, body and spirit. If you don't pay attention to one, it will imbalance the others.

You can use Aether energy to find and release physical blocks, disease or trauma from the physical body. You can also slow down the aging process. As you connect with the Aether inside your body, your energy field becomes stronger. As it becomes stronger, you will be able to develop inner spiritual, healing and psychic powers.

Chapter 5: Mastery of State/ The Breath Method

This method will teach you to become aware of the subtleties of the Aetheric body and the Three Self System. By learning how to alter your state at will, you still the mind and connect with the secret power, raising your awareness of your energetic channels. Breath is the entry point to the world within. As you alter your state, you develop your ability to focus and put aside your chattering conscious mind. You learn how to use the mind and body energies to create a sense of physical, mental and spiritual wellbeing and harmony, to create health and lay the foundations for the advanced practises of healing, manifestation and clairvoyance.

Chapter 6: Mastery of the Body/ Aether Yoga

This increases the amount of vital power in your body. Aether Yoga is a set of simple daily physical exercises that preserve existing Aether and accumulate additional Aether, training and purifying the physical body through easy exercises and postures. They increase your heath, flexibility and strength.

Chapter 7: Mastery of the Mind/ The Mind Method

This method will teach you how to talk to your lower unconscious self. The method brings to your attention how your thoughts and intentions can have an impact on your health and life in general. Again, these simple exercises show you how to alter your state and use your creative imagination so that you can control your emotions and release negative thought patterns that block your success and happiness. Expect to develop positive feelings, open up your heart, and become more enthusiastic and loving towards yourself and others.

Chapter 8: Mastery of the Emotions/ The Spiritual Freedom Method

The method teaches the process of letting go of the past, which frees you up from energetic blocks, clearing the path between the unconscious mind (Lower Self) and Higher Self, which allows you to receive messages from your Higher Self to guide you through your life.

NEXT STEPS

Practice the methods in the next four chapters to build new habits within your Three-Self System, raising your vibration by preserving and accumulating Aether within the body. They will give you better health and greater self-understanding.

Most importantly, they raise your vibration, allowing you greater success in the advanced energy practises of manifestation, healing and other practices.

Becoming attuned to Aether energy will allow you to become more aware of the different vibrations of energy in all living things, from people you meet, to animals, plants and places, even the influence of the energy of planetary movements and the weather.

This connection is a very pleasant and loving connection, and in itself will change the way you view life on a daily basis. You will gain other benefits as well. One thing that happens for many people is the ability to begin to become very aware of the influence of different vibrations on you – how they affect your health, happiness and ability to create your dream life.

Connecting with Aether and building your sensitivity to energy has another very important result. You learn how to raise your vibration at will, drawing in fresh high vibration energy when needed into the body to heal and energise your physical body, or restore your emotions or any spiritual malaise.

Finally, connecting with Aether energy creates clear communication channels between the Three Selves. As the vibrations of Aether flow easily from self to self, you automatically remove any obstacles that block the Aether channels that link your Three Selves. You can then communicate with your Higher Self and the highest parts of the spiritual universe at will. You can use this to receive the wisdom of the Higher Self, to heal and manifest: transforming every part of your physical, mental, emotional and spiritual life.

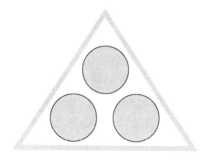

CHAPTER FIVE

MASTERY OF YOUR STATE: THE BREATH METHOD

Throw open the gates, put self aside, bide in silence and the radiance of the spirit shall come in and make its home.

– Guan Zi (trans. Arthur Whaley)

In this chapter you will learn ways to connect with Aether by altering your state using the breath. This is the first way in which you can begin to connect with Aether energy and clear your path of any blocks that stand in the way of total transformation of the self. This method starts to change your relationship with energy. You will find that by altering your state, you find it easy to sense and connect with Aether and establish a clear connection through to the Higher Self so you can access its wisdom.

Every ancient practice practises methods for altering the state in order to access psychic, healing and spiritual abilities. All these practices recognise that if you want to create any kind of intentional change in your life, the fastest way to do it is through trance or meditation. Just regularly relaxing and practicing awareness of the breath tunes into the highest vibrations of love and Aether. As you do this, limiting thoughts, beliefs and energies start to release from your Aetheric body. Your emotions are calmed, your body becomes healthier and the channels between the selves begin to open. Tuning in regularly through the breath method starts to change your vibration, changing your life, circumstances and life.

How to Take Charge of Your Future

Matter vibrates at a lower rate than spirit. The highest realms of spirit vibrate at the highest levels of vibration. This means that in order to connect with the complete power of Aether, you need to be able to change your vibration at will. You do this by changing your state. Changing your state changes your vibration. Every would-be magician or seeker of a greater truth needs to be able to slow down their conscious mind to tune into the Aether vibration.

The easiest and most natural method of connecting with higher levels of Aether starts with the breath. This is the practice of every major spiritual discipline on the planet. Changing your way of breathing creates alchemy inside the body. It changes lower and denser vibrations of Aether into higher or more subtle vibrations of Aether. This allows you to connect more easily with your Higher Self and Spirit. We think of Alchemists as wanting to turn lead or metal into gold. This is the real alchemy. Like a chemist, we can turn something with little value into something of great power and value.

AETHER AND THE BREATH

As you are born, you draw in a first breath. When you die, you end your life with a last gasp of air. Aether enters us with the breath and it leaves with the last breath. Aether is linked with the air element, and breath is the physical medium bringing air into the body to keep you alive. On this earth, we physically breathe in oxygen. However, it is just an earthly element. The vital Aether power is the spiritual essence that combines with the physical element to give you your continued life. As you breathe in, you inhale in Aether with every breath within oxygen. So with every breath you take, you are connected to all other life forces and all parts of the universe, from the smallest creature in nature to other parts of humanity and to the Divine, or whatever you choose to call God. The Aether you are breathing in is connected to every dimension and every realm. This is shown in the language that is used across the world, linking breath with the life force. In the Christian tradition, God breathed life into the earth. In fact, the name of the first man, Adam, comes from the word "Adama," which means "earth." Indeed, in the Christian Old Testament the life force is called "Ruah," which translates as "the Breath of Life."

In Greek the breath is called "Pneuma." Ancient philosophers believed that life began and ended with breath. In India, Prana is said to flow through the nadis, which are subtle veins of energy. Yoga teaches how to accumulate more vital energy through breath work. In China, qigong (which literally means "manipulation of energy") teaches similar practices through breath and physical exercises. The great Chinese philosopher, Mencius (372 BC to 289 BC) was an expert at "nurturing one's breath" or "yang qi." He believed it was vital to all physical and mental practices.

Taoist alchemists, Tibetan, and Indian yogis have for centuries used meditation and magical techniques including breathing exercises to cultivate vital energy for healing and spiritual power.

In Islam the word "Nafas" means both "breath" and "God's breath." So energy is more than a chemical composition like air. It is a divine energy from Spirit and thus we live and breathe because of Spirit.

Among some Native Americans, it is the winds that give life to all living things. They are sometimes called the Holy Winds, and are sacred sources of healing. The aborigines in Australia also work with vital energy for healing and even telepathy.

The idea of the soul across many cultures is also linked to the word breath. The idea is that the two exist together because our souls come from God's breath. Without breath the soul can not be bound into the sheath of the physical body. It would remain as a subtle body, unable to exist in the dense material world in which we live.

In Hawaii, the name for powerful shamanistic healers and keepers of Huna magical knowledge is Kahuna Ha, which means "keepers of the breath." The sacred breath in Huna is called "Ha." Ha breathing like many other forms of sacred breathing in yoga and meditative practice allows you to change your vibration and so gives you an immediate connection to the magical powers of Aether.

Changing state through the breath

While we are in a normal state, the energy in our bodies is depleted through our eyes. In an altered state such as meditation, we turn inwards and our minds go inwards. In this state your vibration is raised and you can create a better connection with your unconscious mind. You connect to the source of energy and fill your energetic bodies with higher frequencies of Aether. You achieve clarity and a higher vibration, and bring restorative Aether energy into your physical body.

There are many ways to help this process happen. Some traditions start with years of preparation of the physical body to allow you to raise your vibration. Others chant or use rhythmic drumming to change the vibrations in the environment, which allows a person to tune in and raise their vibration as well. Meditating and quiet contemplation are also effective. Why these all work is because each of these methods get the conscious mind out of the way so that we can get a clear telephone line, as it were, through the unconscious mind to the Higher Self. This lets our thoughts about what we want flow through the Aether at the right vibration frequency.

The Breath Method gets you to practise altering your state so that you can become comfortable connecting with different vibrations of reality. This prepares you for the manifestation and healing methods in Part Three.

Deep breathing is the easiest and most natural way to achieve deep states of consciousness. Through this mechanism, a kind of alchemy can take place. Deep breathing raises the vibration of the energy within the physical body, opening up channels between the Lower and Higher Selves. This lets you tap into the higher vibrational energies of Universal Aether. By doing this regularly, the channels between the Lower, Middle and Higher Selves are cleared of blocks and obstacles, allowing great benefits to the health of the physical body, healing of the emotions and laying the foundations for higher magic.

Deeper States of Consciousness

When you alter your state you can access the Alpha, Theta or even Delta states: the states of deep relaxation. In normal waking life we spend a lot of time in what is called Beta state.

In Beta state, brain frequency is at fourteen cycles per second.

In Alpha state, the brain changes frequency to between seven and fourteen cycles per second. At this level of mind you will be able to detect subtle energies in a different way than normal.

Deepening the breath can take us down further to Theta state, with four to seven cycles per second. This is a state in which you will be able to connect more easily with higher frequencies of Aether that allow spiritual insights.

In sleep you are normally at one-half to four cycles per second brain frequency, known as Delta state. At this level of frequency, you have automatic connection to the highest levels of Aether flowing through to your Higher Self. Your Higher Self acts as a guide sending you messages in your dreams.

AWAKENING THE BREATH: THE METHODS

Stop and observe your breathing for a moment. Does it feel open and expansive, or restricted and shallow?

Your body carries huge amounts of tension. It's a natural result of being in a high-stress world that has become more and more separated from the natural rhythms of nature.

Just observe your body for a moment. You may have stress in your shoulders, hands, face, jaw, tongue, lower back and stomach. When you carry stress, you block the natural flow of your breath and start to breathe more shallowly. This tension flows from body to mind and from mind to body.

Learning how to breathe deeply helps you physically, and at a deeper level, it frees up the flow of Aether in your system, helping you mentally, emotionally and spiritually as well.

Altering your state raises your vibration. As you change your vibration, thought can flow easily though the Aether from the conscious mind to the unconscious mind and eventually through to the Higher Self. The more we raise our vibration frequencies, the more we send clear thought through the Aether to the highest levels of Spirit. As clear thought reaches the Higher Self, the Higher Self takes the thought and brings about our desires.

In the advanced Aether methods you will learn ways to use the breath to accumulate a charge of Aether, which you can use for healing, clairvoyance and manifestation.

Aether Sensitising Methods

Every Breath method begins in the same way:

▲ Sit/ Stand
▲ Centre
▲ Relax
▲ Feel the Breath
▲ Feel the Aether

Exercise: Two-Minute Aether Connection

This next exercise allows you to feel the energy of the Aether already in your system. You can do this exercise at any time in order to quickly alter your state.

▲ Timing: For practice, you may just want to spend a few minutes doing it. However, it is such a pleasurable state for you to be in that it is highly beneficial for you to do this for up to twenty minutes a day, twice a day.

▲ Benefits: If you do this, you will notice changes in your mental, emotional and physical health, and you may begin to pick up messages in the form of images and pictures from your Higher Self. You will also find it easier to get in touch with your instinct at times you are not in a trance/ mediation state.

PRINCIPLES

You can start to change your breathing in a very simple way. Just by observing the inhalation and exhalation of your breath, you will begin to undo restrictions in the natural flow of breath throughout your system.

First, sit quietly. Find a spot where you are not going to be disturbed. This will only take a few minutes, so you can do it at any time. However, when you first do it, it is easiest to do with your eyes closed, so don't do it when you are driving or operating machinery.

Keep your spine straight. You can sit or stand, but the first time you do this it will be easiest to do it sitting. Let your arms relax.

Now focus on your breathing. Take a deep breath in letting your breathing relax down to your core so that it flows into the bottom of the stomach. You don't have to force this at all. In fact, as soon as you relax you find that the breath starts to deepen naturally.

Now follow these seven steps to relax completely.

THE METHOD

Let your whole head relax. Feel the muscles of your face relax. Let even the skin on top of your head relax.

Let your shoulders relax. Deliberately push them up and let them relax right down again.

Put one hand on your chest and the other on your belly. When you breathe deeply you breathe like a baby, feeling the stomach move BEFORE the chest.

Let your chest relax. Allow your breath to deepen.

Allow your back to relax. Let every muscle and fibre of your back totally relax now.

Send the relaxation down your legs right down to your toes. As you relax notice all your tension running out of the soles of your feet into the ground.

Relax mentally. Let all unnecessary thoughts just leave your body. Breathe naturally.

Even though you can do this relaxation in just two minutes or so, you can find great tranquillity within. As your breath relaxes your body, you will find a point of stillness deep within you. This is you connecting with the higher vibrations of Aether. You don't need to do anything else. Simply notice yourself inhale, then follow your breath as you exhale. Sit quietly and observe your breath for a few minutes. You will notice that your mind naturally becomes stiller and your body begins to let go of some of its tension.

Just doing ten breaths in the morning and ten breaths at night will have a huge effect on your life.

Exercise: Practising Deepening the Breath

To stimulate energy flow in the body effectively, the breath must take place in the lower stomach. Most people breathe in a shallow way, from the chest, leading to tight shoulders and a tense mind. Deep breathing not only relaxes body and mind, but also builds higher vibrations of Aether in the body.

If you have never breathed from your stomach before, it takes practice. After all, you need to break old habits, as normally you breathe entirely outside your conscious awareness. This exercise, along with the Yoga and Mind Method exercises, will increase the habit of deep breathing if you don't find it easy to breathe naturally from the stomach.

THE METHOD

Lie down so that you can fully feel the breath. Make sure you are wearing loose clothing.

Relax and take a few breaths to release any tension from your body.

Now rest the palm of one of your hands just below your stomach so that they are resting on the Dan Tian point.

Breathe in and out through your nose.

Deliberately push out the stomach forcefully and sharply as you exhale, only using the stomach. Make sure you do not involve the hips or other parts of your body.

Pull in the stomach as you inhale.

Repeat this movement with the stomach as you exhale again. Keep doing this, creating a wave movement with the repetition. Start each exhalation slowly and then push the breath out. You should be able to push your hand outwards, using the breath within the stomach.

This practice establishes a habit of deep breathing. After a time of consistent practice, it becomes a habit.

After practice you can breathe deeply more easily standing or sitting. When the habit is formed, you can remove the hand from the stomach area.

Exercise: Bringing Fresh Energy to your Dan Tian Core

Here is another exercise you can add if you wish, to make you even better at breathing and connecting with Aether. This next exercise starts to bring together the body and mind in one smoothly functioning energy system.

Let's start with the breath again. You are going to connect with a strong flow of higher vibration Aether and learn to bring it into the body to deliberately accumulate energy within key points of the body. Sit straight again and in a place where you can be relaxed.

PRINCIPLES

Start by setting your intention clearly in your mind. Remember, this is a thought universe. Your conscious sends your intention as an instruction to your unconscious. Your unconscious hears it and obeys it. If you set the intention to have a particular experience the unconscious will, with repetition, get better and better at giving you this experience.

Use positive language to yourself – ("this is what I intend" rather than "I don't intend xyz"). If on the other hand, you have a negative picture of not succeeding, that's exactly the result you'll get back.

THE METHOD

Set the intention that you are opening up the channels between the Three Selves with the power of your breath. You may also add in other intentions as your intuition tells you.

Sit quietly and relax your breathing. Let every part of your body relax

Now I want you to focus on bringing the higher vibrations of Aether energy down into your body so that you raise your vibration, opening up the channels of the body to vital loving energy. Imagine the Aether entering you like white loving light through the top of your head and descending into your body so it fills up every cell of your body. It flows in from the top of your head and through the major channels of the body.

The breathing, as it relaxes, finds its own rhythm. As you relax more deeply with every gentle breath you can begin to notice a change in the feeling of the world around you. Time and space feels different to you. Notice the change in the feeling of the energy in you, and outside you. You may feel that your sense of separateness with the world changes, and in its place is a sense of connection.

As you breathe deeply and relax, just notice a change in your sense of energy in your body. You may feel a change in the vibration in your body, or perhaps a sense of heat or coolness. You now have a clear channel between your conscious and unconscious minds.

You have a powerful energy centre within the body around the stomach area in which you can accumulate higher vibrations of Aether, rather like charging up a car battery. As you become sensitised to the change in Aether energies within your body, you can bring fresh energy to your stomach area, or more accurately the point just two inches below the navel: the Dan Tian. You can think of the energy in the Dan Tian like the roots of the tree. As you feed the roots, the rest of the tree will grow strong. Your body and mind and spirit are all fed by this energy, which you are now storing in the Dan Tian.

Take a deep breath in, and keep now in your mind the words "Dan Tian." Let other thoughts just drift away as you continue to focus on the Aether energy within this energy centre.

You may at this point visualise the Aether symbol with its three circles, surrounded by a red triangle. See it in your mind's eye over the Dan Tian filling up with energy. This symbol will contain the energy at the core.

After doing this for seconds, minutes or hours – however long you wish – just take an intentional big breath and bring yourself back to normal everyday awareness.

Open your eyes and look around. You may find that everything looks and feels different than it did before. This is because you have accumulated a different vibration of Aether within your body, so you are reacting to the world differently. You literally sense differently, because you are using this extra sense you have.

It doesn't matter how much sense you have of connecting with the Aether power at this time. The main point is that you have set a new intention. This is picked up by the unconscious mind and transmitted to the Higher Self. Whatever you do and intend is rewarded by the Higher Self.

When your breathing becomes practiced you will feel the energy gathering in this part of the body in the form of heat. This is a sign to you that you are connecting with Aether within the body.

NEXT STEPS

Practice the two-minute connection method regularly as a form of meditation. Add any of the additional exercises to it to enhance your practice.

By altering state regularly, you will start to open up the channels between the Selves. Altering your state regularly will begin to permanently raise your vibration frequency, and you will begin to attract different people and circumstances into your life WHETHER or NOT you deliberately carry out the later manifestation and healing methods. This is because as soon as we alter our vibration, we gain access to the higher forms of Aether from the Universe.

You can connect with this power inside you simply, immediately and safely. The more often you do it the better you will get at it. Your unconscious mind loves habit and ritual. Practice regularly and it will begin to understand that you want to create change in your life, and you will get better and better at what you do.

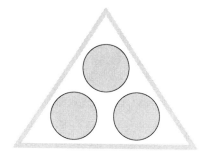

CHAPTER SIX

MASTERY OF THE BODY: THE AETHER ENERGY YOGA METHOD

Life needs motion — Aristotle

Gaining mastery of Aether energy within the body serves three main purposes. First of all, it clears harmful energetic blocks that stop the free flow of Aether power in your mind body spirit system. If you don't clear these they eventually can cause ill health or a feeling of continual stress, tiredness or imbalance.

Secondly, a daily energy practice ensures that you stay healthy physically as well as mentally by training your body to preserve and accumulate high vibrations of Aether power. This leads to short- and long-term benefits.

As you practice the Aether Yoga methods in this chapter you will build the flow of energy in your body and balance your energy. After a short time, you will find that you begin to feel healthier and even younger.

In the longer term there will be even greater benefits. Most practitioners of the exercises within Aether Yoga believe that you will increase your lifespan as a result of regular physical energy practice. The exercises will have an effect on your physical health, and also your feeling of mental balance. If you are someone who sometimes gets stressed or depressed, you will find that there are also benefits to doing regular energy exercise, as you will feel happier and uplifted.

The third reason to practice is subtler, but even more powerful in its effects. The more you practice Aether Yoga, the easier you will find it to connect with and perceive energy changes in the body. You gradually attune to what the Chinese call the energy winds inside the body. These are the subtle movements of energy that change according to your emotions, thoughts, daily intentions and environment, as well as seasonal cycles and other factors such as the food you are eating. As you build this ability, you'll find that you also become much more attuned to the channels between your mind, body and spirit, sensing when one part of your Three-Self System is out of balance.

You will reach the point at which you can easily scan your body for energetic blocks at the smallest cellular level. You will increase your ability to heal yourself and others. At the same time, you will tune into your higher purpose with greater ease. As you raise your physical vibration and your energy channels are cleared of blocks, your Higher Self finds it easier to send you messages in the form of spontaneous insights to help you in your daily life. This also lays the ground for magical, manifestation and psychic Aether work in the next chapters.

The more you practice physical Aether development, the more wisdom you will gain about yourself. Along with the other Mastery Methods, Aether Yoga will allow you to make much more attuned decisions about what is right for you in your life. So each day, take another small step to harmony and happiness by awakening and accumulating Aether in your body.

The power of energy exercise

Healing through movement has been used in ancient civilisations such as China and India for thousands of years. It has always been understood by the ancient cultures on the earth that your life energy will be enhanced if you regularly practice a form of physical movement that makes the body stronger and more flexible. In China, practices like qigong (energy manipulation) have been used for at least three thousand years of recorded history, and are used today by around ten million people. In India, forms of yoga have developed over a similar time period. Some forms of exercise were used to develop strong muscles. Others had a dual purpose: physical health and also "internal alchemy," the ability to change the energy vibration within the body.

Some of these exercises were kept secret for millennia. These include Chinese Daoist qigong (Taoist ch'i kung) health-preserving exercises which were not allowed to be passed on to anybody who was not of a strict heritage. This is because these exercises were so powerful that they could eventually be used for magical purposes, using the Aether energy accumulated within the body.

I have tried all sorts of forms of exercise over the years, often resulting in injury. After many years of doing muscle-building exercises, I learned that they are very different from internal alchemy energy-building exercises, even if they appear to be the same on the surface.

While physical motion is good for the body, not all methods of exercise are good for everybody. Some muscle-building exercises may harm older people, for example. However, the Aether Energy Yoga exercises can be positive for you whatever your age with proper practice.

Some of the energy yoga exercises come from this Daoist tradition of internal alchemy qigong (neigong), which helps every part of the body. Through regular practice you can master your body from the inside out until you are in control of the health of every cell and organ.

In fact, these traditions believe human beings were supposed to live for over a hundred years in radiant health, and can do so using this type of exercise. This is made possible because energy yoga moves energy around the internal channels or meridians of the body in order to preserve youth and health, and to prevent both physical and mental imbalance.

At the same time, the exercises clear the three Dan Tians (stomach, heart, and head) – the energy containers of the body that flow energy to your bottom, middle, and upper half and open up Aether flow in the six directions (down, up, front, back, left and right) within the body.

They complement the Breath Method, helping to build better breath habits, releasing toxins and avoiding shallow breathing habits that can affect your health, while allowing you to cultivate your ability to sense and guide energy flows.

The exercises are very simple and gentle movements that are suitable for most people: tapping, shaking, stretching and very gentle circling joint rotations. Doing them regularly stimulates and restores the energy points of the body and cultivates stronger amounts of energy in the body. Tapping is specifically designed to release energy blocks and help the accumulation of energy in the main energy centres of the body. Shaking and circling lets the body find a natural rhythm that is in tune with the basic rhythms and vibrations of nature.

Notice the benefits for yourself.

THE AETHER ENERGY YOGA EXERCISES

Pay attention to:

The Importance of Smiling

Whenever you do any kind of energy exercise, do it with lightness in your heart and a smile. Smile as much as you can during the day. Wake up in the morning and smile into your body. If you have a picture on your mind of the anatomy of the body, you can imagine smiling each morning into your organs, sending loving energy through your meridians and to each of the key parts of the body that make it function efficiently: the liver, the kidneys, the stomach, the adrenal glands, the heart, the gall bladder, the spleen.

In Tibetan and Taoist practices, it was recognised that this simple action had an impact on what they called the inner winds – the energy inside the system. Why it does, of course, is because of the mind/body connection. Thought is carried on the Aether to every part of our anatomy.

The Importance of Intention

Intention is key to energy and the results you get. As you know, what you think affects the vibration of Aether and where it flows to.

So as you do any of these exercises, keep the intention that they will increase your overall health, energy and longevity.

Also, be clear in your mind that they will help you to get rid of not only blocks to physical health, but also release mental and emotional blocks.

Preparation

You can practice these exercises at any time, all in one go or individually. The Lower unconscious self likes repetition and regularity, so the best way to learn anything new is to practise little and often.

The effects of these exercises are cumulative, so doing some Aether Energy Yoga once a day will let you see a difference in your energy levels quickly. However, if you can spare a few minutes twice a day you will see even faster results.

Avoid exercising just before you eat or straight afterwards. Ideally, allow an hour after you have finished eating to practise. If you feel sick, dizzy or nauseous, simply sit down or come to a standing relaxed pose.

These are easy relaxed exercises, and so should suit most people. In China, it is older people you will see in the park in the morning, happily doing qigong and keeping far more flexible and healthy than elderly people in the West. However, if you have any doubts please do consult a medical practitioner.

Timing

According to the Eastern way of thinking, different parts of the body repair themselves at different times of day. As a result, some times of day will yield better health results than others for exercise. In ancient times, the best times to do exercises were thought to be from 11a.m. to 1 p.m., or from 5 p.m. to 7 p.m. If you are an early riser, then another time you can exercise in the morning is from 5 to 7 a.m. However, do wait at least 15 minutes after completing the exercises before you have breakfast.

BASIC PRINCIPLES

SITTING

You can change the flow of Aether in your system and the health of your body by the simplest of changes. Many of us have to sit for work, so how you sit has a huge impact on you.

In Tibet, sitting was considered one of the most important forms of yoga, because of the importance of the spine as a link between the Lower and Higher selves. If you keep this central channel open during the day by keeping an erect stance, it allows free-flowing energy through one of the most important energy channels of the body. In Tibetan practice it was also considered important to keep the shoulders relaxed. If you begin to hunch in your shoulders, you constrict the energy point in the heart and block off loving energy outwards to others.

STANDING

When standing, keep your legs apart at about the width of your shoulders and your tailbone tucked in. Keep a straight spine and keep your body centred, with your knees relaxed and a strong core at the Dan Tian point.

FOCUS ON THE DAN TIAN

All of the Energy Yoga exercises keep an awareness of good posture with a focus on the Dan Tian point just below the naval. An awareness of this key vitality centre builds balance and power. Poor posture on the other hand, harms this area and thus harms the life force within the body.

BREATHING

Even without doing specific breathing exercises, it is important to breathe in a relaxed way as you move the body. Pay attention to your exhalation, and let the inhale happen naturally. Soon you will find your breath deepening, building up the energy in the stomach area. Focusing on deep breathing is a key part of any internal energy exercise.

AETHER YOGA PROGRAMME FOR HEALTH AND LONGEVITY

PART ONE: AETHER STIMULATION

Power Tapping – Exercises for activating energy and opening up the channels.

Tapping or slapping the key energy points and channels in the body helps preserve good health if it is done as a daily routine. It is a simple physical therapy that helps your Aether flow within your body, and boosts the immune system to preserve good health and stop pain from developing. It lubricates joints and improves the blood circulation. Boosting the energy of the Aetheric body and physical body, tapping can even help structural pain such as back pain, as well as general levels of vitality.

In this simple routine, you rhythmically tap the Aether energy field. You do tapping using the flat relaxed palms of your hands, your fingers or your fists. Use a steady patting motion as heavily or lightly as you like. I do this in the morning. It really warms you up on a cold day, and it sets you up for the Swimming Dragon and other exercises.

Morning body tapping

Stand up straight with your legs apart just a bit wider than your shoulders. Relax the whole body. Make sure you relax and drop your shoulders. Smile as you tap/ slap and send love and energy to all your organs. You are awakening your organs and energy channels letting them expel old stale energy.

Allow your hands to begin slapping your body in a relaxed manner with a bit of momentum. If you count your taps aloud it also stimulates the energy centre at the throat and is beneficial energetically. However, you can also count silently.

THE METHOD

Dan Tian.

Start by tapping or slapping the Dan Tian point. You can find this by first finding your navel, than putting three fingers horizontally UNDER the navel. The lowest point is your Dan Tian. You can tap here for as long as you like. This practice brings energy down into the core of the body, charging the internal batteries. Tap the stomach Dan Tian point, then the side of the colon, then the liver by slapping the right side and then the left. Finally, rub your palms around the stomach in a clockwise direction to stimulate the digestion and prevent constipation.

Upper body.

Tap your shoulders. This helps to prevent stress and frozen shoulder. Then tap down your arms with your palms facing upwards. This activates the heart and lung meridians on the inside of your arm.

As you move down the arms, tap around the inside of the elbows, then work down to the hands and along to your fingers. Then clap the hands together to stimulate the key energy point on the palms of your hands.

Next, turn your arms over, tap the point between your thumb

and forefinger, then tap along the outside of the arm up to your armpits. By doing this you send energy to your lymph nodes, protecting you against breast and lung cancer, amongst others.

Tap your shoulders again to let go of all the stress you carry there. Now, with your thumbs facing up, tap down the arm to the hand, then tap the reverse side from the little finger up to the shoulder again. You have tapped four sides of the arms. Now you can tap the four sides of the other arm. This tapping frees up the flow of energy in the meridian.

Heart centre. Next, tap the heart area to stimulate this energy centre. Use both palms or fists. You can tap up to two hundred times if you wish. Tapping this energy point is good for preventing heart disease, and it also stimulates the thymus gland.

Back. Next, tap your buttocks, again up to a hundred times if you wish. This is a place where stress is stored. Tapping prevents and cures sciatica and problems in the hip area.

Kidneys. Then, move up a little and tap and rub the kidneys vigorously. By stimulating these points you help strengthen the whole kidney meridian as well as the lower back. The kidneys are a core energy system for the body.

Legs. Then move down the front of the legs, stopping at the energy point between the big toe and the toe next to it. Move back up the legs, and then tap your hips. Now move down the legs again on the outside of the leg, then back up on the inside of the leg to your groin. You can do this as many times as you want, but bend down slowly with your head down as you slap, and when you stand up again bend up slowly, bringing your neck and head up last. This will keep you from feeling dizzy.

Head. Now it's time to focus on the head. Tap the back of the neck and then go up to the top of the head and tap there on the master energy point of the body – this opens up your connection with higher energy. Tap the right and left sides of the head. Massage your ears to stimulate all the acupressure points there.

Finish by rubbing your *palms* together until they are warm. Then wash your face with your hands. Rub your palms all over your face, down to up, to stimulate all the points and start your day feeling fresh. Tapping the head area can prevent headaches, and beautifies the skin.

Saliva. Find the saliva in your mouth, wash it round your mouth and then swallow. It is full of healing energy.

Shake the stagnant energy out. End by get rid of the bad energy by shaking out all the stale energy from your body. Brush off the energy from your neck, shoulders, arms, chest, back and sides, then down your legs. Lift your feet and shake the energy out. It is a great way to start the morning and leaves you feeling energized for the rest of the day.

Night Foot Tapping

Do this once a day, ideally at the end of the day. This helps to build up health throughout the body. Sit upright or crossed-legged. Relax your body and mind.

THE METHOD

Rest your right foot on the opposite knee. For women, it is best to start with the left foot.

With a relaxed arm and hand, lightly tap or slap the arch of the foot with the palm of your hand. In doing this, you are stimulating two key energy points in the palm and in the foot. When you slap, do the action as if you are clapping the hand on the foot. It should be a very relaxed movement though you can slap as hard as you want.

Repeat the clap anywhere from fifty to one hundred times to have full effect, with about a second between each slap. Then change foot and knee and repeat on the other side. This opens up the energy points. After you establish the routine, you can reduce the number of taps to around 50 a day.

This method is used in Chinese qigong practice to help yin-yang energy imbalances in the body, and specific disorders such as insomnia, headaches, back pain and depression, amongst others. It particularly helps the heart, kidney and liver. It is a simple but extremely effective exercise to do on a daily basis.

Daily Power Shaking

Shaking the body is something most shamanistic practices do to help to raise the vibration of energy within the Lower Self body mind system. If you have a CD of traditional drumming, just put it on and move naturally to the rhythm. This wakes up the body's energy and brings it into a healthy rhythm. Move around, dance, shake out your body. It is positive to do this at any time. If you want to do a more specific exercise, you can integrate this into your daily programme.

Stand with your feet at shoulder width. Keep your feet parallel.

Let your body gently shake out from your feet upwards. Relax all the joints. Let your breath release. Shake out your arms and shake out old, stagnant energy.

Now let the shake encompass your voice. Let your throat relax. Make a hum or any sound that comes naturally out of your mouth as you shake stagnant energy out of the throat chakra. Let the sound gather momentum filling your whole body with its vibration. Let it fill up your Dan Tian and go right into the ground. If you are healthy, let the shake become stronger. Shake your head from side to side. Feel the shake go all the way down your body.

Finish by standing still. You will feel the change in the vibration of your body.

PART TWO: YOGA

There are many movements that can be used to circulate and accumulate increased energy in the body. Some programmes require you to learn a series of complicated movements. These few simple exercises alone, though, will have the effect you want.

PRINCIPLES

First make sure you have good posture. Then, as you do these exercises, think of being young and keep a smile on your face. The intention of this will carry through every cell of your body.

Energy is about movement. However, the difference between these exercises and exercises that are about building muscle is that you don't strain as you do them. Instead, be soft, rounded and flowing in your movements, just like the movement of energy through your body. Imagine in your mind, as you do these exercises, that you have no bones in your body. Just relax and be soft. Let them happen without effort, and flow freely.

You don't need to do these exercises all in one go. They are simple once you have done them a few times, but don't overreach yourself. Break them down. Do them bit by bit. Essentially, enjoy the process. Remember, energy in the Lower Self is stimulated by physical movement like the breath, as well as the mind. Your intention of enjoying the process has as much of an effect on your cellular level change as does the exercise.

Once you have practiced over a period of time, go back and check the instructions. Check your posture and make little refinements where necessary.

When you begin, you may have a tendency to tense the muscles rather than relax them. Just correct yourself as you go along. As the movements become more familiar to you, it will become easier to stay relaxed.

Do these on a daily basis if you can, and wait at least an hour or so after eating.

PREPARATORY EXERCISES
Basic Vitality Posture

This basic posture is a great way to start your daily routine of energy preservation exercises.

Stand straight with your legs apart at shoulder width. Let your arms relax by your sides. Relax your body and mind.

Take a couple of deep breaths in through the nose. Let your stomach fill up with air. As you breathe in, open up the chest and lift your heels off the floor.

As you exhale, let the heels drop back down. Keep your knees relaxed and slightly bent.

Now you are going to raise your vibration by allowing the body to begin to shake gently, swinging from side to side in a relaxed manner, all the time keeping your arms by your sides. Do this for a few minutes. Feel the whole body, inside and out, shaking.

Now rotate your shoulder blades one by one in a twisting circle. Circle the left shoulder up and to the front, and then back round. Then circle the right shoulder in a backwards circle. This squeezes the body and the internal organs, removing blockages and allowing a healthy flow of energy in the body. Repeat this movement for a minute or so, making larger and larger circles.

This exercise is wonderful for preserving the youth of the body. It helps the internal organs, and is also great for back pain, weight and sexual energy.

Basic Vitality Exercise Two

Simply squatting down and then standing up again activates all the meridians of the body and helps to bring fresh energy into all the muscles of the body. Do this for a few minutes each day and notice the health benefits.

Main Exercise: The Swimming Dragon Rejuvenation and Health Exercise

I discovered this exercise in the 1990s in China. At that time, qigong was becoming more popular, after a long time when many of these powerful exercises were kept secret. Even now, though, there are very few great qigong masters. This exercise comes from the once-secret Daoist tradition about energy and is used to promote rejuvenation and longevity. This particular exercise comes from a sect of Daoism from Huashan Mountain, one of the five holy mountains in China and a key energy centre in the world. Since it is easier to learn this exercise by seeing it, take a look at the several versions of this exercise on YouTube and the internet.

In Eastern tradition, many energy exercises ask you to mimic the actions of animals from tigers to phoenixes. In this exercise, the dragon represents the energy moving through the body. A swimming dragon flies up to the heavens, gathering energy from the heavens and coiling down towards the earth, bringing energy down. You can imagine the dragon playfully moving with its tail swinging through the body.

The whole body is used in this exercise. In the exercise, you make three circles with the palms of your hands joined together along the front of the body. Your arms circle around the top of the head; then, as you sink the body down, the hands circle around the middle part of the body and then the lower part of the body (as if each major energy part of the body is being charged with fresh energy). Then you allow the body to rise up again. As you go down and up again, your waist swings left then right, so every part of your spine moves and every organ feels the movement as well. In the final movement, you rise up on your toes and stretch upwards.

This exercise has been used for thousands of years to create health and longevity. On a physical level, it increases blood flow and stimulates the endocrine system. It also counters the dropping of the base metabolism rate that occurs in older people. It is great for weight reduction, helps pelvic slackness in women, makes the back strong, reduces the size of the waist and boosts the strength of the kidneys. It also acts on the elasticity of the skin on the face, through stimulating hormones.

PRINCIPLES

Keep a relaxed posture. As you do the exercise, let go of tension through the body. Let your head be light on your shoulders, as if it is suspended from the top of the crown chakra point from an invisible ceiling attached by an invisible chord.

Keep your weight equally between your two feet. Let your body weight move downwards. This causes the Aether energy to circulate within the body and stay within it, rather than being released. When you bend your knees and raise and lower your heels, this stimulates the kidney, liver and spleen energy channels.

Don't worry if this exercise isn't totally smooth to begin with. You can gradually make this exercise into one beautiful, flowing, long, smooth movement. Make sure you use your whole body, tracing complete circles. As you do this, your spine makes S-shapes, opening up the vertebrae like a gentle chiropractic movement. This helps the flow of lactic acid. As you move, your bottom swings in the opposite direction to your hands. This is called "shaking the tail of the dragon."

If you want to see amazing changes in your life, practice this exercise first of all for twenty minutes a day. Each cycle will take around a minute. The more you do, the more energy you will create flowing through your body. You can then start doing more than one cycle a day.

Instead of doing it as a morning practice, if you have a job where you sit down a lot, do a few cycles as a break after you have been sitting for an hour or so. It will help you prevent getting a bad back and give you an "energy shot."

However, do at least some energy practice. Breaking the habit will make a difference to how much energy you build in your system. If you want to lose weight you can do two twenty-minute sessions a day. Your digestion will be improved, and your weight should be gradually normalized.

Let your breathing be regular; you don't need to think too much about it when you are first learning this form of movement. Breathe from your stomach. Keep the Dan Tian relaxed throughout. Keep your spine long and straight so it can be a pure conduit for the energy.

Make sure your palms and thighs are pressed together throughout the exercise in a relaxed way so that the energy stays in the system as you do the movement. The fingers of the hands remain closed.

Remember to smile!

THE METHOD

Start by standing up straight. Keep your feet together, with your ankles almost touching each other. Keep your knees soft and not locked. Keep your hands by your sides with the fingers pointing down. Your weight is centred. Find a point of equal weight between the back and front of your feet by shifting the weight back and forth until you find the point between the ball of the foot and the heel. Bring your attention to your lower Dan Tian.

Relax your mind and mentally scan your body, checking where

is tension. Let your breath relax. Deliberately relax your shoulders and anywhere else that habitually holds tension. Let your breathing come from your stomach. Keep your tailbone tucked in to straighten your spine.

Bring the palms of your hands together in front of your stomach. Then, keeping your palms together, rotate them upwards so that they assume the prayer position.

Bring your hands up just below your chin, keeping them in the prayer position. Now, moving your hands slowly, all the while with your palms pressed together, tilt your head to the left and bring your hands alongside it, as if your head is almost resting on your hands. Your right hand will be uppermost, palm pressed on palm.

At the same time, the entire top half of your body tilts to the left, causing the hips to swing to the right. This creates an S-dragon shape in the body. As you tilt further to the left, let your arms extend further out and up, making a semicircle around the top of the head.

As they reach the mid-point of your head, your body swings back in line so that you are facing forwards with the arms but your legs and hips are straight. At this point, your face is slightly down and your hands are facing forward at about the level of the crown of your head. Your waist is slightly forward.

Now complete the circle by moving your arms around to the right so your head comes to the right and your hips move to the left to balance the movement. Your spine moves to the right and you end this part of the movement with your left hand above the right, palms pressed together.

Now it is time to begin the second circle. Continue the movement by turning your hands over, keeping your palms pressed together so that your fingers now point to the left at about the level of your chin. Your right arm is parallel to the ground. Turn your head very slightly to the left side.

Move your hands at the level of your chin to the left. Let your knees gently bend so that you start to sink down in your body. The hands stay together as you trace a circle in front of the upper part of the body. Your hips shift out to the right. As you draw near the close of this circle, your left hand is on top and your thumbs are facing forwards. For the finish of the semi- circle, your hands point downwards at the level of your solar plexus.

For the third circle, the body's centre of gravity continues to lower. Draw a semicircle along the lower right side of the body. The left hand will start on top of the right. Let your hips roll to the left as you do this. As you trace the circle to the right, your hands turn over so your right hand is on top, still palm to palm, and your knees are deeply bent so you are in a semi-squatting posture.

This completes the movement from top to bottom. Now it is time to move from bottom to top to complete the three circles. To do this, you simply reverse the process.

Move your hands with palms pressed together from the left side, tracing a semicircle in front of the lower half of the body. Roll your hips to the right, let your head face the right, and move your hands up and to the left, up to the level of the solar plexus. As you do this, begin to straighten the body, bringing up your centre of gravity. Finish in front of the solar plexus with the palms facing down.

Trace the middle semicircle with the palms of the hands pressed together, moving your hands towards the right. Your knees continue to straighten. As your hands trace the circle, your right hand moves to the top and your hips swing to the left.

As your hands reach the top of the circle, your right hand is on top with the fingers pointing to the left at the level of your chin.

The final circle in front of the head is made by moving your hands, palms together, to the left, around the side and then above your head. Roll your hips to the right as you make the circle, and then back to the centre. As you reach the central point of the circle, your head is forward and your palms are stretched upwards together above your head, as if your are praying above your head.

Rise up on the balls of your feet, making sure your bottom is pulled in as you stretch your arms up and your whole body stretches to follow it. After a few seconds, lower your heels and lower your hands to the prayer position in front of your heart.

Finally, bring your palms to rest on the Dan Tian, making a triangular cradle for the energy centre by resting thumb on thumb and first finger touching first finger. Let your breathing relax. Over time you will feel the contact between the energy flow in your palms and the energy accumulating in the Dan Tian.

ENDING THE YOGA PROGRAMME
Close-down exercise

Because you have stirred up energy in your body it is important to calm down afterwards, as you have excited the energy in the body through the swimming dragon exercise.

Dan Tian Breathing

It is very beneficial to do Dan Tian Breathing for around five minutes after completing your yoga programme. You can sit down in a mediation position with your hands resting on your legs and palms upturned or lie down.

THE METHOD

Focus only on your Dan Tian just below your navel.
Inhale for about five seconds and let your stomach inflate.

Exhale and let your stomach muscles pull in as much as possible.

This method accumulates energy in the Dan Tian. At the same time, the movement of the stomach muscles gently massages and activates the nine meridians that go through the stomach area, which helps the kidneys, spleen and stomach, amongst others.

SUMMARY:

Six Reasons to Practice AetherYoga

Practising this form of yoga regularly will help you to preserve your physical health and also give you a feeling and appearance of greater youth. This is because this type of yoga helps to balance hormone levels and restore the optimum functioning of your organs.

It may also help you lose weight and help your sexual energy, as well as boosting the ability of your immune system to ward off illness.

Long-term practitioners of energy yoga systems like qi gong are said to live longer.

At the same time, as the exercises build physical health, they also build your ability to access deeper states of consciousness. On a basic level this builds relaxation and release stress, helping you to balance your emotions.

On a more fundamental level your vibration is raised as you build your ability to stay in every moment of "the now." At the deepest level this will help you to clear blockages from the channels between the three selves so that you harmonise and centre your physical, energetic, emotional, mental, and spiritual being.

Strong energy in the body gives you better results in healing, manifestation and clairvoyance as well as overall spiritual growth, awareness, inner knowing and authority.

NEXT STEPS

Practice regularly and you will begin to see changes in your mind and body as well as your overall levels of energy. Although the changes may be subtle at first, clearing the Lower Self of blocks to energy flow on a regular basis will cleaning out obstacles that allow you to carry out feats of manifestation and healing. You can add into your program any qi gong or Indian Yoga exercises, or exercises from other disciplines such as Aikido, if you wish. Please of course do check with a medical professional that you are healthy enough to begin this exercise programme before you start.

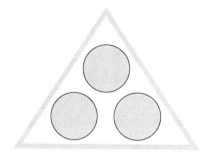

CHAPTER SEVEN

THE MIND METHOD: MASTERY OF THE MIND

You create what you focus on, so focus on what you most desire
— Anonymous

Through the Mind Method, you will learn how to check any negative effects of thought within your energy fields. You will be able to identify and release dense negative energies from the system, and flood your system with higher vibrations of energy through higher vibrations of thought.

Thought affects the health and energy of the body. What you are thinking has a moment-by-moment effect on every part of your energy in every cell. If you have a tendency to talk negatively to yourself or feel negative, your unconscious will pick it up. These thoughts will stay as energetic thought forms in the Lower Self.

Because of the mind-body connection, the effects of your emotions and beliefs you have about yourself have an effect on both your physical appearance and health. At the same time, these thought forms block your ability to do higher forms of magic such as healing and manifestation.

This method builds on the Breath Method, "clearing your path" and teaching you to alter your state intentionally to create new energy connections between the Three Selves free of obstacles. This will allow you to receive clear messages from your Higher Self about anything else you need to which you need to pay attention.

The Mind and Energy

Let's start by looking at how what you think affects you not just mentally but also physically. The mind-body connection is a very powerful thing. Whatever you are thinking will be reflected in your emotional and physical health. This can be demonstrated in a very simple way.

Ask a friend to do this little exercise with you. Get your friend to stand straight with one arm extended out parallel to the floor. Face them and put a hand on their shoulder so they are kept stable. Now ask them to resist with their raised arm as you push firmly down on the arm. You will feel the resistance and then the "give" in the arm as you push down.

Next ask your friend to think of a flow of energy through the arm, as if it is a hose with Aether flowing through it right through the fingers in an everlasting flow. Test the arm's resistance again. You will find it much more difficult to press the arm down, as the resistance will be stronger.

There are two final tests to do. First, get your partner to think of a time when they felt really positive or happy. This creates strong resistance in the energy field.

Finally, ask them to think of something sad. Test the arm again. It will be easy to push down. The negative thoughts depress the vibration of energy in the system, making the energy field weak.

THE MIND METHOD

The Mind Method is very simple at heart.

- ▲ Sit/ Stand
- ▲ Centre
- ▲ Relax
- ▲ Feel the Breath
- ▲ Focus

Allow your creative imagination to work for you at the deeper levels of mind, clearing away what is not needed and receiving messages from the Higher Self

The Mind Method uses the power of the breath to alter your state, then takes the breath method a stage further to create an active meditation in which you can give clear instructions to the unconscious mind to clear out blocks.

You use thought every day, whether you are aware of what you are doing or not, to affect your body, mind and emotions. The Mind Method uses the power of thought to intentionally create change in your life so that you can restore harmony in every cell of the body. The goal of the Method is to continue to open up the connection between the Selves by clearing out unwanted emotional habits and negative self beliefs. Once these are cleared out, the Aether can flow freely.

Your Lower Self loves to help you. One of the ways it does this is to follow your instructions as best it can. Learning how to talk to your unconscious mind is very important because it is the only direct link each of us has to our Higher Self. Any improvements we want in our lives will depend not on what we want consciously but how clear our unconscious is.

This method is a way of clearing blockages from your mind and body whilst in a relaxed state. This is similar to self-hypnosis or trance, and is the best way in which you can have good communications with your unconscious. You can clear out old habits and excesses from your system. You can ask for healing to be brought to the cells of your body.

BASIC PRINCIPLES OF THE METHOD
Relax

The mind method builds on all the breath work you have done so far. All you have to do to start the process is to relax, breathing from your stomach rather than your chest. This takes you into an alpha state level of relaxation.

Have a clear intention

When you do the Mind Method, you can just let the unconscious bring an image to your mind to clear, and trust that even if the image doesn't make conscious sense to you, it will clear emotional or mental blocks from your mind. To aid this process, before you do the Method, check for unwanted emotions and negative beliefs. Think: do I have any anger, sadness, grief, fear or anxiety, or any beliefs here that do not support my connection with my Higher Self? Write down specifically what you want to clear by doing the Method. Your unconscious will do its best to do this for you.

Pay attention to your language

Every thought you utter is heard by the shared consciousness of the universe. Be careful to focus on what you want rather than what you don't want. The unconscious thinks in pictures, so if you think about what you don't want, all it will pick up is a picture of that. To give you a quick example, "Don't think of a blue tree." What do you think of? A blue tree! Putting the word "don't" in front of it doesn't make any difference! So use words carefully.

Be Kind

When you talk to your unconscious, be clear and kind. Be loving, and approach this method with the intention that everything that happens comes from the higher good. The Higher Self will support you in what you do.

Harmony of the Three Selves

Whatever other purposes you have for your practice, say to yourself each time you practice: My goal is to harmonize my thinking, conscious Middle Self with my unconscious Lower Self and my Higher Self. I now invite this to happen.

State to yourself your intention that from this moment on you will be harmonizing this flow of energy between each of the selves. As you transmit this thought it starts the process on its way: Lower Self to Middle Self, Middle Self to Higher Self, Higher Self to Lower Self.

STAGE ONE OF THE MIND METHOD

First, sit quietly. Find a spot where you are not going to be disturbed. This will only take a few minutes, so you can do it at any time. Close your eyes.

Keep your spine straight. Let your arms relax. Let your whole head relax. Feel the muscles of your face relax. Let even the skin on top of your head relax.

Let your shoulders relax. Deliberately push them up and let them relax right down again.

Now focus on your breathing. Take a deep breath in, letting your breathing relax down to your core so that it flows into the bottom of the stomach. You don't have to force this at all. In fact, as soon as you relax, you find that the breath starts to deepen naturally.

Allow your back to relax. Let every muscle and fibre of your back totally relax now. Send the relaxation down your legs right down to your toes. As you relax, notice all your tension running out of the soles of your feet into the ground.

Relax mentally. Let all unnecessary thoughts just leave your body. Breathe naturally.

Deepen your state. Imagine there is a flight of ten stairs in front of you. You are going to walk down those stairs. As you count down from ten to one you are going to start moving down those stairs in your imagination, one stair at a time.

As you move down each stair, you will feel more and more relaxed and you will go deeper and deeper into a perfect place of inner stillness and focus, cutting out all external sounds and thoughts so you can just go deeper and deeper.

When you reach the number one and the bottom stair, I want you to imagine that you can see a door in front of you. Take hold of the handle and walk through the door. You may find yourself inside or outside. This is the home of your unconscious Lower Self. It contains many things.Look around you. Scan the place you are. Feel how it feels. You will feel totally comfortable as you do this.

Now you can use your mind to get rid of old attachments within your unconscious. These attachments are emotional or mental thought forms contained in the energy of the unconscious mind.

Now ask yourself the question "is there anything in this place which I no longer need in my life?" If there is, notice what it is. It is likely to be shown to you in the form of a symbol or picture. You don't need to know the exact meaning at this time. When you awaken you can, if you wish, meditate on the meaning.

Notice there is another door or gate that you can see in front of you, which is permanently open. This is the door to the light. Place whatever you want to remove from your space by this door in your mind's eye, and it will be sent back to the light. This will happen immediately. This will clear the thought from your energetic system.

You may also ask for messages from your Higher Self when you are meditating. Messages may come in the form of words or an image.

A. Simply say, "I ask my Higher Self to give me a picture or symbol for what I need to know at this time to grow to my highest good." Or "What else do I need to know to harmonise the three selves?" Again, the answer may be shown to you in the form of a symbol or picture.

B. Your Higher Self may appear in the form of a guide, or simply show you what you need to know through pictures.

Coming back to consciousness

Leave your space and come back through the door. Come back up to waking consciousness by just counting one, two, three, four, five. At the count of five, be fully awake and return to normal consciousness, knowing that your unconscious will continue to clear unwanted blocks out of your life and you will continue to connect more clearly in future with your Higher Self.

Messages from the Higher Self

You can repeat this basic method whenever you need to. Regular practice will create better communication with your Higher Self and your unconscious mind. Even if you don't get messages the first time you use this method, it is likely that you will the next time.

You may be unclear at first what the messages you receive mean. The Higher Self communicates in the form of symbols and pictures. These have either archetypal meanings – i.e. common to everyone – or they will have very personal meanings. For example, you might see in your trance a Spirit Guide of some type appear in the form of a man handing you a wedding ring. If you recognise the ring as belonging to your mother then this is probably a personal meaning. Think about why it was your mother's ring? Is there a particular meaning it holds in your life? What emotional attachment do you have to it?

But if it is just a wedding ring, think about the general idea of being married or weddings or rings. What significance do these ideas have for you? You will find many archetypal meanings of dream symbols in dream dictionaries.

If you believe that the messages call for an action in the real world, then make sure you take that action. If you repeatedly get the same message, then you have not interpreted the message correctly.

Dreaming

You will sometimes find that practising the Mind Method will cause you to dream more actively. This is because the channels have opened up more clearly between the selves.

Be aware of any messages you get from your dreams, and interpret them in the same way.

STAGE TWO OF THE MIND METHOD
Boosting your Life Force through the Mind

As well as emotional thought forms, you can clear out unwanted energetic thought forms in the shadow body of the physical body.

Because our belief in time is so strong, you probably think it is inevitable that you will age. Yet you are much younger than you think, even in this moment of now. Many of your cells are only hours or days old. Your organs renew themselves constantly. Your blood, kidneys, liver, gallbladder, stomach … every organ and every cell is constantly renewing itself without any conscious doing on your behalf. Your Lower unconscious self does this by means of the life force Aether. The Lower Self carries out this function second by second, every moment of your life and every moment of now. In energetic thinking, when you hold youth and health in your mind, your body will be restored according to the picture you hold in your mind.

THE METHOD

Sit or lie down. Using the countdown method in the previous exercise, relax physically, emotionally and mentally so that you raise your Aether vibration, allowing the channels between the three minds to open and allowing your sixth sense to open up.

As you enter the Alpha state of deep relaxation, you can deliberately stimulate your creative imagination. Your unconscious Lower Self loves your imagination. It takes the pictures you make and sends them along the Aether through the chord to your Higher Self. Your Higher Self is waiting to bring these pictures into reality.

Bring into your mind's eye a picture of how you want to look and feel, youthful and healthy. Feel what it will be like, hear what people will say to you, imagine every feature of your new youthful face and your new youthful body.

Set the intention that every day your cells will be renewed, bringing into being this picture. You have a hundred trillion cells in your body. Every single cell carries within it the living intelligence of Aether energy. Every cell in your body is controlled by the Lower Self and waiting for your instructions.

Imagine opening up the top of your head and letting in the highest vibration of universal Aether directly from your Higher Self. Now imagine your new picture floating within the Aether, as if it is floating on a river flowing through your body. Let the picture of the new youthful you drift lazily within the Aether through every cell of your body, until each one of them is filled with fresh energy and fresh thought.

Imagine the Aether flowing now through the meridians of your physical body into every organ and cell, repairing and renewing.

Renew your features of your face, your torso, your arms, your legs with youthful dewy freshness. Visualise yourself just as you want yourself to be. Imagine your skin fresh and young. Modify your face and, as you know it, know it has already happened. The vital power can do whatever you want.

Every cell, system and function of the body is healed. You glow with health, every day feeling better and healthier.

NEXT STEPS

In the next chapter you can practise the final mastery method, which is a way in which you can let go of unwanted emotions and people from your life.

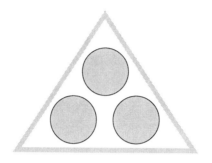

CHAPTER EIGHT

MASTERY OF EMOTIONS AND SPIRIT: THE SPIRITUAL FREEDOM METHOD

The universe is mental, held in the mind of the all
– The Kyballian

This chapter teaches a process of emotional release and chord cutting on an energetic level, helping to let go of false attachments from the unconscious mind. By doing this, you provide yourself with emotional and spiritual healing on a deep level.

Have you ever felt drained by being around a certain person or group of people? Is there a relationship that still upsets you when you think about it, but you can't seem to let go? Or perhaps it's just the daily contact with people at work that leaves you feeling low on energy?

This is because you are being drained of Aether by the contact with the person. Sometimes relationships are stressful or harmful to our wellbeing. Toxic emotions can result from bad relationships, which can then harm our health.

When we meet or even think about other people, we link with them via the aetheric "aka" chords. Aether flows between the two people via these sticky chords. When you think about somebody, you send out a chord or thread which sticks to the other person. All contact, be it physical, emotional and mental, sets up chords between people and things.

The stronger your relationship with someone, the stronger will be the chord. Where the chords attach to affects the relationship. For example, chords going from heart to heart will promote unconditional love between two people. Energy flows along the chords between people, which is fine when you feel loving towards each other but not so good if things have gone wrong. Chords can stay in place after we have moved on. Chords stay from old relationships and maintain old perceptions of other people and ourselves.

Some chords we have dissipate energy. When one person's vibration is lower than another, the person with the lower vibration will take energy from the other unless steps are taken to protect your energy field. It doesn't make a difference whether this is a past or present relationship; unless we clean up our chords, the thoughts will bring energy down. If you split up from a loved one suddenly then the chords yank our heart and pain is caused. In an obsessive relationship there are many chords tangling between the two people. This stops you from being able to move on and inhibits your growth.

Take an inventory

Before you do either of these methods below, think about people you know and how you think about them. Do an inventory. Are you carrying any guilt about the way you have behaved towards anyone? Is there anything you could do in the immediate world to make amends? Actions will also help remove negative connections. If you are carrying any anger, this needs to be released, as the only person it will harm is you.

Chord Cutting

Chord cutting is the process of making things right between people. It is a good habit to adopt, to ensure that you keep your energy clean of harmful links.

When you become aware that you have an unhealthy relationship with someone, or simply need to refresh the energy between the two of you, do this process. You imagine that you can ask for the energetic chords between the two of you to be restored to where they have come from if they no longer serve the highest good of all concerned. You release your own energy chords and connections and absorb them back into your shadow body, receiving back the Aether energy to give back to your system. The energy is cleansed as it returns.

THE SPIRITUAL FREEDOM PROCESS

This process is a good practice to do regularly, even every day. It teaches that all problems that appear to exist are just your perception. In fact, situations don't really exist outside you at all. You can un-create a problem just as you can create a problem.

The ancient healers of the islands of Hawaii knew that shame and guilt and other attachments caused negative thought forms within the Three Selves, which set up physical, mental and spiritual ill health. The Chinese call these false attachments. There are several ways we create these attachments.

When we lie or make mistakes or fail to tell the truth, we feel guilty and bury the feelings inside.

If we are greedy or do things to excess, we harm ourselves and others. If we intentionally hurt another person, the unconscious recognizes it as a sin and our conscience stores it as an attachment. When we judge ourselves for not being perfect and think of ourselves as unworthy and undeserving, failing to give ourselves love, this sets up attachments and negative thought forms.

The ritual

The Hawaiians traditionally used a forgiveness ritual called ho'oponopono to make things right and clear these attachments. In this ritual, you forgive yourself and others. You release all guilt, shame and feeling of "sin" and achieve spiritual and emotional release. It was also developed into a process of mediation within groups of people, in which the causes of the problem were communicated and forgiven.

Many other cultures have similar rituals of chord cutting and emotional and spiritual release. Shamans believed that when you feel on an unconscious level that you have sinned, your unconscious punishes you. Even if consciously you change your mind, your unconscious may still think differently, so you then have a divided middle and lower self. You hold this "sin" in the form of energetic thought forms in your unconscious. This can result in illness or, through the Law of Attraction, attract negative circumstances into your life.

In the ritual below, you use the loving vibration of Aether from your Higher Self to clear blocks out of the unconscious mind, clearing the path and allowing health in your whole system. This process will also help your relationships, even past relationships where you have suffered from pain or grief. It stops these negative emotions being stored in the energetic bodies as thought forms. If you've ever found it hard to move on after a difficult romantic or family relationship, or feel you are carrying other burdens from the past or present, then do this ritual regularly. Remember, the lower unconscious self loves ritual, so the more it does it, the better it will get at it and the better and freer you will feel. Then you can move forward to manifest more of what you want in your life, rather than having to out up with all those things you don't want.

THE METHOD

Close your eyes.

Visualize yourself now growing until you are a one hundred-foot giant. You are all-powerful and can restore everything in your life back into balance on an emotional and spiritual level.

Ask all those negative emotions you have about yourself and any self-critical image you have about yourself – the you that has been formed every time you think "I'm not good enough," "I can't do this," "I'm too fat, ugly, etc." to come as pictures in front of you and below you, as if they are appearing on a small stage. You are not affected by them because they are at a distance from you, and you are larger and more powerful. You have put thought energy into these false images. Once you clear them, your life will begin to change. Ask *all* your unwanted emotions to come into vision. You may see these in the form of thought forms, looking rather like dark patches of clouds in your mind's eye.

At the same time, invite the images of anybody you want forgiveness from or with whom you need to make amends or have unsaid communication with. See your image of these people in front of you now on the stage. Think about ex-partners, family members, friends, teachers, colleagues and anybody you have been in contact with today and this week. You can even do this process around past family ties, asking your ancestors to come forward. This clears any family thought patterns out of your mind/body.

Stay above these images and stay taller than them. You are always a powerful magician. Now, notice the chords that run between you and these people and past emotions. These are chords which bind you together energetically through the current thoughts you have about them, or the thoughts that you have retained from the past.

Now take a deep breath. Open up the crown of your head. Imagine that link to your Higher Self and all the other Higher Selves in the universe opening up, which allows the highest vibrations of love and light energy to flow from the universe into your body. Let the light vibrate above your head and then flood your body. There is so much love and light it can flood out, seeping through every cell of your body and filling the images in front of you with the love vibration as well.

Imagine, as you see everything and everybody fill with love, that you are these people and they are you, because that is the truth. See yourself playing their parts in life. Understand how they played that part. Forgive them for it. Feel love and forgiveness to everybody there, including your past negative emotions. Thank them for their forgiveness. Remember, it is the feeling of love that releases the old emotions and energies.

Now imagine that you can ask for the energetic chords between each of you to be restored to where they have come from if they no longer serve the highest good of all concerned. You can see yourself cutting these chords if you like, with light and love. Release your own energy chords and connections and absorb them back into your shadow body, receiving back the Aether energy to give back to your system. The energy is cleansed as it returns because you have cut the chords with perfect love. Watch the people and images in front of you dissolve into light or drift into the universe as the old energies are dispersed.

The benefits

This is a healing ritual. When you do this process, what you are really doing is forgiving yourself because the energy is really within you. By doing this you take back false projections, you take back your own power and you clear anything that blocks your connection with your Higher Self.

What's the point of wasting energy on not forgiving? When you don't forgive you literally waste Aether energy from your Three-Self System, blocking all the energy pathways so your body can't heal, you can't manifest and you may have physical or mental illness.

You don't need to just do the ritual. Forgive in your mind on a daily basis just by thinking "I forgive him or her." With moment-by-moment forgiveness, your life becomes more loving. Sometimes, when you complete the ritual, you find you immediately hear from the person whose chords you have released, and get a surprise contact within the real world. That new contact will feel totally different because the energetic connection between the two of you has changed.

Once you let go of all these old attachments your life becomes freer and simpler. You will start attracting different people around you through the law of attraction, as your vibration will have been raised. Your Three Selves can now be balanced and integrated, being in perfect harmony.

NEXT STEPS

Now you are ready to create magic!

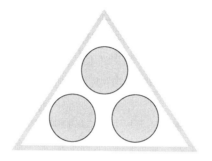

PART THREE

CREATING MAGIC

The Mastery Methods are preparation for other, more advanced practices. If you have practiced regularly, you will have raised your vibration and your general sensitivity to being able to feel or even see Aether energy. You may be able to sense it in the body or be aware of energies coming from other people. You may also be able to tune into a room or place and know whether it has low energy or high, healing energy.

At the same time, as your vibration is raised you will become more aware of your own intuition because it has become easier for your Higher Self to send you messages, as the channels between your three selves are now clearer.

You can take further control of your destiny now by practicing purposeful mediation and energy healing. The ways of manifestation and healing are given in the next chapters. The final chapter lays out some more advanced breathing and state control practices. When you use these regularly, expect to have profound changes in the way you feel emotionally, physically and mentally. You can also use the methods in this final chapter if you wish to attune to your psychic powers.

The more you practice, the more consistent your results will be.

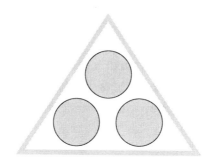

CHAPTER NINE

THE WAY OF MANIFESTING

It matters not how strait the gate,
How charged with punishments the scroll
I am the master of my fate:
I am the captain of my soul.
— Invictus, William Ernest Henley

This chapter will show you how to decide and deliver your own destiny. Using the power of Aether, you can have, be, or do exactly what you want in your life. You can bring into your life things, relationships and people, or new opportunities and circumstances.

Over centuries, magicians and gurus have sought out the secret of how to master the universal power, casting spells and meditating for years to uncover the secret so they could create anything from gold to changes in the weather. As we know, the secret has always been a very simple one. Once you harness the power of thought, you can create your desires. Whatever you are able to believe can be manifested will be manifested. It can happen because the world exists in the mind and the substance that holds the mind or thought is the power: Aether, the vital power that is the life force of the universe.

This chapter will teach you a method by which you can harness this power to change your life from today onwards. Whether you want wealth, health or happiness, a new career, a different relationship or something more, these things can be yours. Magic takes place when you use the power of Aether to open up your link with the invisible universe. By thinking about what you want and willing it to happen, you link in to Aether power and you really can change the circumstances of your life.

How does manifestation work?

The process by which this takes place has been described as a vortex opening up between the two worlds: the invisible universe, and the material universe we can see and feel and hear around us. I prefer to see the process like a telephone call. You pick up the phone and send a thought up through the telephone line of your unconscious to your Higher Self. The thought becomes the spark of creation. It bursts into being in the invisible universe. Then it comes back into matter as what we call reality.

Perhaps you send a picture of your wounded leg healing up, or of you meeting a new boyfriend or getting a pay rise. It doesn't matter what the thought is, it will exist immediately in the invisible universe as soon as you transmit it. Thought travels on aka chords within the Aether.

When the thought is turned into reality in your life, it is

according to the rules of time and space in the material world. This means that although creation happens instantly in the invisible universe, it isn't created instantly in this one. Your new boyfriend does not materialise in your room within seconds. Your pay rise happens three months later and your leg heals within two weeks. You don't actually see it healing in front of you.

What can block this?

If you trust the process and allow for time, your wishes will always turn into reality. However, the one thing that can instantly block the process is doubt. Doubt is ingrained in us. If it wasn't, we would all be creating life as we consciously want it every day of our lives. We would all have perfect health, the relationships we want and the life we want.

Do you remember those old films where to make a call you have to go through a clunky old exchange where an operator plugged and unplugged wires to enable the call? Why does it sometimes feel as if our call for help or change isn't getting through, but is being blocked by an old-fashioned operator somewhere?

When we wonder why magic is not happening as we intended, it is because of your unconscious beliefs and thoughts. However liberated you may think you are in your thinking and living, you may have deep beliefs about your ability to create your destiny. The attitude of your peers and society both act as forces to block you. Deep-held beliefs are hard to shift. If you think you can create magic, you will have a real material effect. You will be able to create healing and manifest real changes in your life. However, if you think you can't then you definitely won't.

The voice of society and authority is very strong in our ears. Social ridicule can stop you from connecting with Aether. That is why many students of magic and mysticism have kept what they do secret over the centuries. Many magicians have used pseudonyms to disguise their links with magical schools and societies.

If they were not defeated by society, they also had to fight their own inner scepticism. From the time we are children, we have ingrained within us the rules of this world. All the possibilities for magic we are open to when we are young are schooled out of us. In order for you to work with the Aether, you need to change your mind, let out those old beliefs and let in the ones you had when you were young. Be childlike in your belief in the possibility that magic can work for you.

CREATING MAGIC: THE BASIC PRINCIPLES OF THE UNIVERSE

Knowledge is power. If you want to create magic – intentionally creating change in your physical self and your physical environment – it's important to understand the operating principles of magic. It's a bit like reading the manual before you start the machine. If the machine doesn't turn on properly or stops after a few minutes, then you'll know exactly what to do next. Understand the rules of magic and you will be able to control it.

You can create magic with the Aether. But be honest with yourself. Even those who think they believe sometimes inwardly don't believe to the same degree. Remember that the whole of your body is enthused with thought. There are over fifty trillion cells in the body. Each cell carries within it, thought-charged by the power of the Aether, vital energy. Therefore, it isn't just your brain that thinks. Each cell of your body carries within in it memory of the past and the perception of the universe as you see it in the present. That's why we do the physical and mental training before doing these manifestation techniques – because they clear old thoughts out the cells of the body and put in their place fresh charges of Aether.

In order to create any "intentional change" in your life, choose your thoughts and actions carefully. This is because in a universe of thought, every thought or desire we have consciously or unconsciously causes ripples in the pool of consciousness around us. You can't but affect the world you live in. Everything you think in the here and now sends out a ripple that seeds a "real" effect in this physical universe. Therefore, every magician chooses and learns to control his or her thoughts.

At the same time, every magician follows universal laws as he or she creates this change. These are the explanation of how and why the magic in the Manifestation Method works. Keep these in mind as you carry out the method and seek to design your own destiny. Also, read again the explanation of the Aether Universe in Part One for more details.

Basic Principles of the Universe

Cause and Effect: Every effect has a cause. Every cause gives rise to an effect. If you repeat an action under exactly the same conditions it will have the same result. It is predictable. An effect can be caused by conscious intent or by unconscious intent. So you affect the world around you whether or not you are conscious of it. As a magician, why not choose how you affect the world by intentionally being the cause of your life? Choose what you want to manifest and use the power of Aether to create positive effects in your life.

Vibration: Everything in this universe has its own frequency and vibration. Its vibration determines the form it takes. If you want to change the form of something in the material world, simply change its vibrational frequency. You can do this for yourself by using any of the Clearing the Path methods, as they will all change the vibration of Aether in your Three-Self System.

The Law of Correspondence and Connectedness: We are not separate from the universe. The universe acts as a mirror, reflecting back your thoughts in real events in your life. If you're not sure what you believe, just observe what's going on around you. See what events and people you attract, to understand where you need to create change, balance or grow in your life. If you notice several things happening around you that have a pattern to them they are not a "mere coincidence." Watch and learn from the clues.

Focus: You get what you focus on in life, according to the Law of Attraction, so focus clearly and precisely on what you want, with complete unison of your conscious and unconscious minds. Be clear to visualise exactly what you intend to manifest. Check your thoughts every day. If your vibrations are low, work on the vibration of the Lower Self using Aether Yoga and the Mind Method.

PREPARATION

Check that you fully have taken on board the operating principles of the universe. When you understand these basic principles, you can begin to intentionally set about designing your life as you wish it to be, becoming co-creator of your life with the universe.

Remember the highest form of Aether energy is the love vibration. It overcomes all other energetic vibrations and it can only attract love back. So if you want love, all you need to do is to open up your heart and give love. The energy will magnetise love back to you. Always make magic with a smile and love in your heart.

Build the muscles of your mind - Learning to visualise and focus

To be able to manifest, you need to be able to visualise what you want to manifest, be it a new car or a new life. Your ability to focus will already have been trained through the Aether breathing and mind method exercises, in the foundation steps in previous chapters. However, regular practice in focus and visualization will also help the accuracy of the results you achieve in the manifestation method.

You can begin this very simply.

- ▲ Just stop what you are doing at the moment. Look at an object near to you.
- ▲ Now close your eyes and see it in your mind's eye as clearly as you can. Scan the object in your mind's eye and remember each detail of it as clearly as you can.
- ▲ Now open your eyes.

How easy did you find that?

A magician learns how to cut out the noise and chatter from his mind, stilling his mind so that he can creatively imagine the life he wants to materialize. Then he uses the power of Aether and the Three-Self Powerhouse System to make this life manifest as he has first imagined it.

You will only achieve what you want consciously if you give your unconscious mind clear instructions. It wants to fulfil your wishes, but if you are fuzzy it will be fuzzy. You first need to train your mind to focus on exactly what you want to have in your life. How easily and clearly you visualise will influence how successfully and accurately you are able to manifest in your life.

Imagine, for example, that you want to lose weight. If you have a clear picture of yourself at a lighter weight and thinner than you are now, the Aether will be able to materialise that picture into reality. It will ensure that it puts into place the circumstances that make the thinner you happen. However, if the only clear picture you have is of you as you are now, at your heavier weight, then that is the picture the Aether will help you to make real and you will stay at this heavier weight.

Being able to sense something clearly in your mind's eye is the skill that will help the Aether to manifest for you.

Pick another object. Look at it.

Close your eyes again and see every detail. Turn it over in your mind. Look at the front and back of it.

Notice every imperfection and flaw. Notice the colour and shape. Now bring in your senses and notice the smell, the taste, the sound of the object. This time, hold the image for at least thirty seconds.

Magicians have always known how important it is to be able to create in their mind's eye the feeling of what they want to bring into reality from an idea into matter. Practicing each day will build up the muscles of your mind, like going to the gym builds up the muscles of your body. Soon you will find it easier and easier to hold an image and focus without strain for several minutes at a time. Make your aim to reach five minutes gently cradling the image in your mind.

As well as objects, practice bringing to mind faces of people. Start with your own face. You see it in the mirror every day, but can you reassemble that picture when you close your eyes? You may find at first it seems a little shady or fuzzy. Look at yourself in the mirror then close your eyes and recreate each nuance, each feature, each part of you until you see you standing there in your mind.

Now you can bring into your mind other people you know, the faces of your friends and family and people you don't know – faces of potential people in your life. Mastering this skill ensures that you send clear pictures to your unconscious of the future you want to create.

Magical Preparation Method:
Charging the body with universal energy

You will need to be able to do this breath in a relaxed way to become a master of healing and manifesting. Ha Breathing comes from the Hawaiian magical tradition. The story goes that when Captain Cook first discovered Hawaii he asked a native, "what is this place." They replied, Hawai'i. He sailed on to another island and asked again. The answer was again Hawai'i. In fact, the meaning of Hawaii is "to live in the mana (Aether) that lives on the life breath." Hawai'i in effect isn't a place outside you: it is inside you.

The Ha Breathing method is a very powerful breath and considered a sacred breath. There are many traditions of sacred breath on the planet. This is the one I find easiest and most effective for quickly building up Aether energy in the system, to allow both manifestation and healing techniques. The word "ha" in Hawaiian has many meanings. It can mean life itself or it means to breathe with some effort. It is more than the relaxed breathing you have practiced so far. A further meaning of "ha" is a trough that water flows through. If we take water as a metaphor for energy, you get the idea that by making the ha breath, we cause the Aether to flow along the right channels. This ha breath causes a surge of higher-vibration Aether in your system, allowing either the magic of healing or manifestation.

THE METHOD

Start your breathing not by inhaling but by exhaling, to let out all the stale air out of your body. As you exhale, let your mouth relax and you will find it natural to make a "ha" sound as the breath is expelled. Squeeze in your stomach and you will expel the last bits of air. Then you will naturally take an in breath and fill up your system again.

Continue breathing, out and then in, making the long relaxed "ha" sound. As you breathe, you find your whole body fills up with fresh air and at the same time your body lets go of stress and begins to relax. To intentionally build up a surge of high-vibration energy in your system, practice exhaling, holding the breath, inhaling and holding the breath. The secret of ha breathing is in the ratios of the breath.

Exhale for five counts, hold for five counts, inhale for five counts, hold for five.

With practice you will be able to take longer breaths and hold for longer. Practice any time even for small amounts of time, when you are watching TV, driving a car or before you go to sleep. Any time you are stressed, simply exhale and then continue ha breathing.

The best way to practice breathing is to do sets of four complete breaths.

THE MANIFESTATION METHOD

Now you are ready for the Manifestation Method. This is a highly effective method of making your wishes into reality. This method is very different from making a wish and hoping it happens. You will be using a clear structure to achieve the results you want by harnessing the power of your Three-Self System and giving life to your desire using the vibration power of Aether.

STEP ONE: SHOW GRATITUDE

Start by recognizing what you have already got in your life that is positive. Count your blessings and say thank you to the Higher Self. This sets up a positive connection between the selves and gets the Middle Conscious Self the cooperation of the Lower Unconscious Self. This is rather like a parent saying "well done" to a child. The child wants to help its parent further because it has received praise and gratitude for what it has done so far. Train your unconscious by rewarding it with carrots, not sticks.

STEP TWO: PREPARE YOUR PICTURE

Picture the result you want clearly, as if it is already in your life. Decide what you want and picture it. You can decide what you want to do, have or be in your life. This sounds simple, but it is where most people go wrong. There is no point just thinking "Oh that would be nice" or "I would quite like to have that" or "it probably won't happen, but I want it to."

Take all the time you need to get really clear about the sort of life you want to manifest. Don't rush the process or you might inadvertently cheat yourself. Remember, though, to determine to create in your life things and circumstances that will bring good to all and not harm others.

Think for example about how you can give service with what you ask for to people you know, to your community and to the world. When you have a broad picture of the future you would like, you can start to bring your desires into reality.

To manifest, you need to take your imagination to a place where you can see the new life you want actually happening to you, as if it has now already been created in your present life. In other words, the picture will carry within it an intention and an assumption that it will happen and be realized in your life. Your unconscious will only have a clear idea of what you want to manifest if you can visualise what you want to happen in the future more clearly than your picture of it not happening. Don't just use your visual sense. Feel what you want as if it has actually happened. Get excited. Feel the happiness, pride, joy or whatever the emotions are that you expect to have. Imagine what people are saying to you now you have this new life.

Be clear

For example, perhaps you want enough money to buy a house? You can imagine having the money in your hand but it's is probable you'll get a bigger buzz when you actually own the house, so picture that house. Picture the keys in your hand as you walk through the door and look around. Feel the excitement as you realize that you won the house. Imagine what you will be saying to yourself. Let your body flood with feelings. Get all your senses involved. Perhaps there will be a lovely smell as you walk through the door, or a warm fire burning in the grate. Who do you want to be there with? When do you want this? Are you alone in your picture or with your perfect partner? What are they like? How does it feel being with them? Use all your senses to flesh out the picture.

Make yourself feel as if your prayers have been answered by God/ Spirit/ The universe/ whatever you choose to call the higher powers. It will feel as if you are pretending at first. The trick, though, is to just keep acting as if you believe that it will happen. Doubt is what destroys magic. As you visualize your future just for a few minutes, be in it without doubt. You did this when you were a child. You used your imagination naturally. Now is the time to find that skill again and use your creative imagination until the feelings come. This is the magic formula, the philosopher's stone that alchemists have always sought throughout history.

Don't be tentative about it. Leap off the cliff to your future and enjoy living in it in your mind's eye. Once you have pictured what you want, with feeling attached to the picture, what you will have done is to create a thought form that can be transmitted to the Higher Self.

This begins the manifestation process involving all Three Selves. The conscious Middle Self decides on the picture and gives the instruction to the unconscious Lower Self. Your Lower Self will do its best to transmit the picture to the Higher Self. The Higher Self infuses the picture with the highest vibrations of Aether and brings it into being in your real material life.

STEP THREE: ACCUMULATE A CHARGE OF HIGH VIBRATION AETHER

The next step of the process is to train the Lower Self to send the picture of what you want in your life to your Higher Self, using the power of the Aether to take it along the chords between the selves.

In order to make this process work, you need to have clean channels of communication between the selves. This allows the flow of Aether to reach the right vibrational level.

To make sure that this happens, at the beginning stages of energy magic, you charge your body with energy through the Ha Breathing method.

After you have made your picture, charge your body with fresh power. Breathe in sets of four for several minutes until you feel your body filling up with fresh energy. Increased breathing creates a charge of high vibration energy throughout the Three-Self System, which acts as a stimulus to the Higher Self.

For some people, the method will become such an integrated part of you that you won't have to add the breath, because you will become so used to changing vibration and altering your state without having to exert effort. If you can do this, then you will open up an instant and easy channel to the Lower and Higher Selves. At this point, all you need to do is to set your intention and it will be carried easily on the Aether to your Higher Self. For the majority of us, though, the Ha breathing method is a quick way to achieve the same result.

Charge the body with Aether – The Method

Stand with your feet slightly apart. Keep your knees straight and hands slightly out with palms upwards.

Exhale stale energy out of your body using the ha breath. As you breathe in, feel light energy filling up your body.

Now you are going to do four groups of four complete ha breaths (exhale and inhale). This creates a very strong charge of Aether.

Be relaxed in your breath so you build up fresh energy without hyperventilating.

You will begin to feel focused and clear minded as your whole system is filled with the ha breath, bringing in the fresh higher vibrations of Aether. You don't need to visualise the energy flowing through your Three-Self System; your unconscious knows exactly what to do with it. However, if it helps you to have a picture in your head, you can visualise your Higher Self as a ball of white light floating above your head.

STEP FOUR: POST YOUR PICTURE

The next step in the manifestation process is to intend that the thought form you project is carried by the charge of Aether in your system through the chords connecting the Three Selves to the Higher Self.

You have charged your body with ha breathing. This brings about an altered state. See your picture energized with Aether energy pouring down from the universal source. Then see it dropping into your future. Ask your Higher Self to take care of this for you and choose the right point for you. As this happens, it will be accompanied by great pleasurable emotions.

STEP FIVE: SAY THANK YOU

As you complete the process, in your mind or out loud say "thank you" to your Higher Self and the universe for already being in the process of bringing your desires into reality. The Polynesians say "Let the rain of blessing fall."

The reason you do this is because it is not enough just to have a desire that what you want to manifest is manifested. The key is to turn your desire into an expectation throughout the process that you will succeed in your endeavours. Be without doubt and expect that your Lower self will carry out your commands. As you thank the universe that this new future has already been realized, you recognize that this new reality is in the process of happening and is now replacing all other realities that existed prior to this.

Remember the Higher Self is UTTERLY TRUSTWORTHY. It will do what you ask it to do if you are clear in your intent. For this reason, it is very important that when you visualise a new future, you intend that this be to the good of all concerned in your future.

Know that your thought form is being carried along the Aether to your Higher Self. Your old future is being torn down now. Your new future is already a memory within the highest levels and vibrations of the Aether, so it is already linked with the futures of other people around you, your family, your partner, your children. If you change your future, you need to intend that any future that replaces the old one comes in a form that is to the highest wellbeing of all these interlinked people.

And, always ask that when what you want manifested occurs it does so "In the way which is to the highest good of all concerned."

STEP SIX: CHECK YOUR PATH IS CLEAR

Your prayers will always be answered if you have cleared your path. If they are not manifested, you need to keep sweeping those energy blocks away so that the higher vibrations of Aether can charge every cell of your mind, body, spirit system and let the magic take place.

How do you know if there are obstacles?

If you can't feel positive pleasurable emotions about your picture of the new present, it may not be the right future for you, or you may need to clear any blocks or attachments in the unconscious and clear the path between the Selves.

First check: Is this future what you really want?

If it is not right, throw your picture out and start again. There is no point compromising. Feel your reaction to what you think you want. Really check and check again for the feeling.

If you are adamant that you do want a particular result and yet it consistently fails to manifest, you need to check what is going on unconsciously. Your conscious wishes may at times be in conflict with your unconscious wishes. It may be that your Lower Self is not able to carry your picture to your Higher Self because the path is still blocked.

For example, suppose you want to stop smoking but nothing is happening. You may think you want to stop, but your unconscious knows you get a lot of enjoyment in the present from smoking. It is not going to listen to your instructions for a new future unless the feeling attached to your imagined future picture is stronger than the feelings it gets from smoking in the present.

Check again – what do you really want in your future?

Fear, shame and guilt as well as anger and hurt can also cause blocks. These emotions need to be cleared. The Hawaiians thought that the Lower Self has to believe that it is worthy to approach the Higher Self. If it feels unworthy in some way, it hides itself like a child that expects punishment from an adult. The more reward you give to your unconscious Lower Self, the more it will feel worthy to deliver your prayers to your Higher Self. The way to do this is to constantly reward the Lower Self by setting up new positive rituals. The Lower Self loves rituals. They make it feel loved and safe. Clearing the path is an ongoing ritual for the Lower Self. So set up the habit and continue it. Start a lifelong practice of change.

As well as being able to manifest your desires, you will be happier and feel more harmony in every part of yourself.

SUMMARY:

First, prepare the ground. Make a list of what you think are the blocks in your life. Know what you need to get rid of, including habits, emotions and people. Intend as you do this that this will only happen if it is to the higher good. Clear your environment. Get rid of things you don't need. Complete what needs to be completed. Get rid of your physical baggage to let go of some emotional baggage.

Then use the Mastery methods to further clear your path of blocks.

Clear negative thought forms from the unconscious through suggestion when you are in Alpha State. For this you use the Mind method.

Work directly on the physical body to clear energy blocks from the body. This frees unwanted thought forms directly from the cells of the body. Using Aether Yoga will help you to do this.

Do the Spiritual Freedom process to clear negative attachments with people or emotions.

Finally, just going into alpha state regularly with the breath method will keep the channel to your Higher Self open. Use the breath method to regularly alter your state so you can listen to what your unconscious wants to let you know. Notice what thoughts and images spring into your mind while in a trance/ meditation state.

There is also one more method. You can use the Manifestation method directly as a way of clearing your path. Instead of asking for something to be manifested, ask for the attachment to be cleared. Create an expectation that this will happen.

STEP SEVEN: MAKE IT A HABIT

Each day, spend a few minutes just focusing on the picture of what you want to happen having already happened. Imagine that the time has come when what you want has already happened, and flesh out your picture. See your future as it will be when it exists looking through your own eyes, feeling the feelings you will be feeling, hearing what you will be hearing as if it is happening to you right now.

The manifestation method may be repeated daily if you wish. If you have an attitude of total trust, then the desired results will come simply from setting your intention. You won't even need to alter your state or build up an additional Aether charge. However, beginners will find that they may need to overcome social conditioning that denies magic exists, and can be done by anyone. Repetition of the method keeps it active in your unconscious. The Kahuna shamans of Hawaii saw this rather like watering a plant. The thought forms you have created through your pictures of your intended future are like seeds scattered into the consciousness of the invisible universe waiting to grow into wonderful plants. You can't see them growing, but they are there ready to pop up into your life when it is right. By sending fresh Aether through a daily practice, you water those seeds until they are ready to become real.

SUMMARY OF THE PROCESS

Here is the manifestation method in summary.

Your conscious mind/ Middle Self has the responsibility for the decision about what you want to create in your life. You decide carefully whether you want wealth, health, a happy relationship – any new condition in your life. At the same time, count your blessings to get your Lower Self enthused with what is to come.

Visualise what you want in as much detail as possible and you will create a set of thought forms around the new desired results.

Clear the path. Ask for the cooperation of the Lower Self and make sure it is clear of attachments. You do this by really noticing how you feel about the future. If you are incongruent you won't manifest it. Take clear to bring to attention what needs to be cleared, and use the Spiritual Freedom Method as well as Aether Yoga and the Mind Method to clear the channels between the selves.

Ask that the Higher Self choose the way of manifesting that is best for all involved.

Make your future picture real by charging it with the life force of Aether. You make sure that when you do this the vibration of the Aether energy is high by breathing in universal Aether using the sacred ha breath. This ensures that it can reach the vibrational level of the Higher Self. You can also ensure that you build up supplies of Aether though regular breathing practice, the Mind Method and energy yoga.

Review the results you want regularly. Repeat the manifestation method with freshly charged Aether daily if you wish.

USING THE AETHER SYMBOL TO MANIFEST

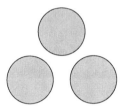

The Aether symbol can be used for manifestation to add power to the process on a daily basis.

Ground and build energy each day. Visualise the symbol in red at your Dan Tian then mentally draw a triangle around the symbol to ground it.

Feel the energy channels open through each of the circles within the symbol. Visualise the circles joining to become one as the Aether flows between them.

Now visualise a second symbol in front of your third eye. It is likely to be either white or violet. Your Higher Self will let you know the right colour for you to use at this time.

Open up your crown chakra and let universal light flow down through the top of your head through your third eye and through the symbol. This acts as an amplifier, expanding the energetic force. Imagine that the picture of what you want to manifest is in front of the symbol. Energy flows into the picture expanding and energizing it.

Do this for a few seconds.

SUMMARY:

This is a highly effective method of cosmic ordering or magical manifestation – the most powerful I have ever found. Practice with it and experiment with it and make it your own.

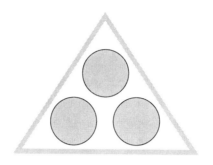

CHAPTER TEN

THE WAY OF HEALING

Unless the study of esoteric science yields fruits of practical application, it is unworthy of the pursuit of any serious minded person, and unless these fruits be the fruits of the spirit, it is unworthy of the study of any spiritually minded person.

– Dion Fortune

Aether healing is based on the idea that all healing is self-healing. You can use Aether to heal your own energy or to influence the energy of other people in a positive way. Energetic traditions believe that this will make a difference to your health and the health of the other people with whom you practice energy healing. Please note however this is not a substitute for medical treatment of any kind.

My first experience of receiving healing energy was very positive. I felt energised and calm. However, when I first learnt to give healing I felt very drained. This is the experience of many people who practice forms of spiritual and energy healing, or indeed, people who care for others feel drained after they do so. This is because they are using their original vital energy rather than channelling universal Aether energy. Chronic fatigue syndrome and other disturbances to the health of the body are supposed to result from draining your original energy.

Some healing systems, like Reiki, do tune directly into universal energy, but require specific attunements by a Master of the system. The Aether system does not – you can use it immediately today, though you can also enhance healing using the Aether symbol of the three circles.

The Aether healing techniques in this chapter are very simple ways of doing what I have learnt over a lifetime. You can use them immediately for healing by tuning into this energy in a very powerful way.

Benefits

Energetic healing aims to help the physical health of the body, as well as mental and spiritual health. There is no limit to the healthy state you can achieve through the Aether because the universe holds the potential for anything to be realised. The only limits will come from your own social conditioning and the beliefs you have about what is possible. Your Three-Self System has unlimited power and potential.

Energy and Health

Why is it that in general, children have much more energy than adults, and as you get older you seem to have less and less? Most of us take our bodies for granted when we are young. We party. We miss out on sleep, we feel pretty immortal. When you are young, if you fall over, you seem to heal fast. But then, usually around mid-life, health problems can materialise. Older people just seem to take longer to heal, and sometimes they don't. Before long you're dragging yourself out of bed with joint pain, low energy and niggling aches and pains. This is because the life energy becomes depleted over time unless you do something about it. You can. You were born to be a healer. You can heal yourself and others.

As every cell is connected to universal intelligence through the Three Self System, each cell of your body knows how to restore and repair itself. People who have developed their extra-sensory powers through gift or regular practice will be able to sense, feel or see disturbances in the shadow bodies where the Three Selves live. For example, if you have a wound on the physical body, there will be a corresponding wound within the immediate aura. If you have a strong negative emotion that has built up over a long time, it will hang as a thought form shape attached to the shadow body, and if it is not removed will result in illness.

Sometimes, clairvoyants can see colour changes, greying or dullness of the shadow bodies which indicates that the Aether is depleted, and unless fresh universal Aether is brought into the body, illness results.

Healers should pay particular attention to the energy centres of the body that bind the shadow body to the physical body.

Certain practices such as Tantric Sex ensure that vital power is not lost to the system though the loss of semen, which depletes original Aether. In Tantric practices you can also gain vital energy through your partner.

We also gain vital energy when we turn inwards through mediation. Quiet mind, peaceful attitude, practice gives health and long life. For health in the mind and spirit it is the same.

Environmental healing

Aether is present in our environment. Being around nature helps us to receive additional energy. The sunlight also contains Aether. Sitting outside in the sun brings fresh energy into the body. Because the Aether contained in sunlight is so potent, drinking water that has been in the sun fills up the body with energy.

The Earth contains its own Aether, and we link into it through the energy points in our feet when we walk barefoot on the earth. This helps the energy throughout the body, as well as a feeling of groundedness that also helps the ability to focus and work with a clear head.

You gain Aether from the water you drink and the food you eat. The vibrational quality of Aether within them will be affected by where they come from. For example, fresh food will have more Aether in it than food that has been stored for many months. Water that has been exposed to a lot of sunlight and unpolluted environments will have more Aether than water that hasn't. You directly take on the Aether from what you eat and drink, so choose wisely and eat seasonally where possible. Because the vibration of Aether can be changed by thought, however, if you don't have access to fresh food and water, just the process of being grateful and loving to the food and water before you have your meal will change the effect it has on your body. Get into the habit of saying thank you for what you are about to receive, and what you have eaten and focus fully as you eat rather than multitask or watch TV. It will have a measurable effect on your health.

SELF HEALING

If you are helping someone else to energetically heal, you are not the person who is doing the healing, you are only the medium for the Aether to do the healing.

Illness results from blockages to the energy flow in the body. Disturbances caused by blocks in the shadow body of the physical body disrupt the internal channels of the body. The body generally renews itself at anything between days and months. A small cut generally repairs quickly. Large wounds, diseases or injuries to the body may take longer to be healed. For healing to take place, the body needs life energy to heal itself. Healing can be accelerated by upping the vibration of the body and removing blocks to healing. This can speed up the self recovery process.

THE WAYS OF HEALING

There are two ways to work with healing the body of illness or disease when working with another person. Both ways work equally well, because the mind and body are perfectly connected by the energy of Aether Power.

If you are using healing energy for another person you can use a hands-on method, bringing higher vibrations of life energy into the affected area. As you touch each part of the body that needs healing, your hands channel Aether energy. This acts like a healing poultice to the area, as the healing you send through your hands raises the vibrational field of energy around and within the body.

You can also project the healing energy through thought energy – the distance or mind healing method if the person is not present. With this method you build high vibrations of Aether energy in your body, then with your mind you direct energy to where it is needed using the channels of energetic aka chords between you and the other person.

PRINCIPLES OF AETHER HEALING
Keep a clear intention

In both methods, as you heal you need to hold in your mind a clear picture of what it will be like when the healing has taken place. In Hawaii the kahuna or shamanistic word for this was ha'ha'o, which meant "putting a thought form into something."

What you do when you work with another person in this way is thrust a positive thought form or picture of healing into the consciousness and shadow bodies of the patient using the force of your Aether energy. You will automatically raise the vibration of the Aether you project. The negative thought forms and emotions are of denser energy, and are forced to remove themselves from the shadow body. When the blocks are removed, energy flow in the body is increased and acts as a catalyst to the natural self-recovery of the body.

Self healing

For self healing you can also work internally, visualising the healing of the affected part of your body, instructing the lower unconscious self to heal the cells of the body. This may involve sending instructions to the lower unconscious self to remove mental and emotional blocks that have caused the physical problem because of the mind body connection.

Hand positions

Generally, when you project energy through your body, keep an open palm. The energy comes from the central point of the palm (the lao gong acupuncture point) and the fingers in a broad beam of energy. You can also point a narrower beam of energy through one or more fingers.

Timing

How long you need to project energy for will vary enormously depending on the patient and condition. You can spend anything from five minutes to an hour on a patient. Listen to feedback from the other person about what they are feeling. Also use your observation. Pay particular attention to changes in breathing and skin colour. If the breathing is relaxed it is fine to continue but if the patient's breathing starts to get shallow it is time to stop. When healing is working the skin colour remains even.

Long-term conditions will need regular treatments, probably once a week over a period of months.

HEALING BASIC HANDS-ON METHOD

You can use the basic healing method for physical illness or for healing emotions or mental imbalances in the body.

Stand up straight. See the energy point at the top of the head that acts as a direct channel with universal Aether. See Aether as a white light or the light of the sun filling up the shadow body, in which the Lower Self lives around and inside your body.

Ha breathe for several minutes until your body is infused with fresh energy. Four rounds of four complete breaths should be a minimum. Sense the Aether filling up your whole system.

Now stand behind the person who needs healing. Hold a picture on your mind of expectation that the healing will take place. Your mental picture will be sent to your Higher Self, which links to the Higher Self of the person who needs healing, so your expectations of what will happen will have a direct result on what takes place.

Set your intention. Say to yourself "I am now sending universal Aether energy directly to xxx person in order to heal and make perfect again (what needs to be healed) so that they be restored to full, natural health." Keep holding with purpose the picture of the person in full radiant health.

Now place your hands directly on the person who needs healing, either on their shoulders for general healing or on the specific place where there is a problem. You can also heal the major chakras of the body. If it is more appropriate, hold your hands an inch away from the body, as the shadow body will still be healed without directly touching the physical body.

Picture the Aether flowing through you like water, or a stream of white light flowing where it is needed. It helps if you have a picture of the channels or centres of the body in your mind as you do this to keep your intention focussed and clear.

The surcharge of Aether will directly transfer to where it is needed.

You can also use this method for yourself and for plants or animals. You will notice that if you treat some plants and not others, the ones that receive energy grow better than the ones that don't.

Take care. Only keep the picture of the condition when it has been healed. Don't use any words describing the illness in your mind or carry a picture of the problem, or the Aether will transfer this picture to your Higher Self as the result you want for the patient.

For example, say to yourself, "I am flowing pure Aether energy through my hands in order to cause your weight to return to your natural light weight of your youth," or "I am flowing pure Aether energy through my hands to make your eyesight perfect."

Resistance to healing

If you find resistance to healing, the way to overcome it is to accumulate an extra charge of Aether. As you send the energy to where healing is needed, state your intention in your mind to use this extra energetic force to overcome all negative influences and expel them from the Aetheric body. State your intention to only do what is to the highest good of the patient.

If you want to do this for yourself, state your intention that you are now putting this new thought form or picture of yourself healed in your mind to replace any previous negative thoughts. Intend that you stay in perfect health at all times, physically strong and active and young in mind and body.

USING THE AETHER SYMBOL

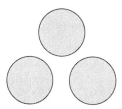

Symbols and talismans are powerful tools to aid healing. A symbol is a thought from infused with energy. When enough people use any symbol for healing and loving magical purposes, its vibrational power is amplified and amplifies your healing work. The more you put your thought and intention into the Aether symbol, the more effective you will find it as a tool to enhance your healing. It can also be used as a tool for clairvoyance, as you will see in the next chapter.

As you carry out the basic healing method, imagine the basic three-circle symbol over the body of the patient or in the palms of your hands. Draw it in your mind from top to bottom, and draw the circles clockwise.

To complete the symbol and ground your energy force, visualise the symbol. Then, in your mind's eye, imagine that you are painting a triangle around it, signifying the unity of the Three-Self System.

The colour of the completed symbol is likely to be violet or rich blue for emotional healing, and red or orange where physical illness is present. Again, let your Higher Self be your guide to the right colour for you at any particular time.

ADDITIONAL HEALING TECHNIQUES
The violet flame

The violet flame is an ancient energy symbol that has been used for many years for healing. As such it is a very powerful thought form. You can use this flame to cast out negative thought forms and attachments from the body where you feel extra power is needed.

Sit and relax. Breathe deeply with your eyes closed so that you enter your alpha state.

Now bring into your awareness the Aether energy. See it and feel it building into a flame of violet light energy. Bring the flame all around your body so that it caresses every contour and every cell. Bring to your awareness the thought forms that are of low vibration that are preventing you from being at your most magnificent.

The violet flame is a light loving vibration, so these dense vibrations can not resist it. They do not belong to your body. They are not part of you. At some time you learned to bring them into your aura, so now you can expel them from your body.

You may see or sense names for these vibrations. They are likely to relate to significant negative emotions and negative self beliefs. Let the violet healing flame unhook these thought forms from your Aetheric body and burn them away.

Let the name of the thought being unhooked come to your conscious awareness and the flame dissolve it so that it turns into light. All unhealthy emotions and negative thoughts are now leaving your body.

If self-limiting thoughts arise, you can transmute them with the flame.

Distance healing

If you are not in the same place as the other person you can still send healing energy. You can work with a photo of the person, sending energy at a distance through your hands directly laid onto the photo.

If you don't have a photo, write the person's name down on a piece of paper and send energy to the person either through laying your hands on the paper with the name.

Aether Distance Healing Method

Ha breathe for several minutes to charge your body with fresh energy. Four rounds of four complete breaths should be a minimum (see BREATH METHOD).

As you do this, become aware of your heart centre.

Visualise the person who needs healing standing in front of you.

Open up your crown centre to allow universal energy to flow in a constant stream through your body.

Now extend a chord from your heart centre to the heart centre of the other person. Allow the healing energy to flow through you to the other person, and intend that it is used as needed to heal and make the other person free of blocks at any level and in any body.

When you sense the time is right, detach your chord and close your Crown chakra. Ground yourself by bringing your focus down to your Dan Tian centre below the navel. If you want to, you can also imagine roots running into the ground bringing your energy back down.

You can do this method with your eyes closed or open. This method can also be used to send healing to animals as well as people, even to plants.

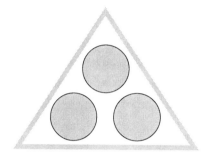

CHAPTER ELEVEN

THE WAY OF TRANSFORMATION

If you would like to go on to develop your powers further, use the methods in this chapter. They will make you become more aware of many things – the different vibrations in your environment, messages from your Higher Self. You can also use your powers for further transformation of self. Some learn to use their powers for telepathy.

PREPARATION
Advanced Breathing Methods

All of these methods will help you become an advanced master of the breath and thus of the energy. As you gain heightened sensitivity to the secret power, your Higher Self will guide you to what changes to make in your life and you will receive daily messages of wisdom through your intuition from the clean energy channels between your three selves.

"Standing Post" Meditation

In ancient times in Egypt, China, Africa and the Americas, standing meditations were used as a way of changing consciousness. Standing meditation is a way of developing a still mind and awareness of the circulation of energy in the body. It has been used in some cultures to induce dreams, clairvoyance, healing powers and soul journeying.

The ancient hunters used standing meditation as a way to increase their awareness and tune in with nature and their environment. In the Standing Post meditation, you learn to stand as strongly as a solid post fixed into the ground. As you stand, your awareness of everything around you grows. This is a wonderful meditation to learn because it is active and passive at the same time. As you stand, you change state inwardly and at the same time you build up strength in the legs and waist.

The best time of day to practice this is in the morning for about five minutes a day at first. You can build this time up over several weeks.

THE METHOD

Posture

Stand up straight with your feet shoulder-width apart. Keep your weight evenly distributed between both feet, and let your weight be evenly distributed so your feet are firmly rooted into the ground. Your toes face straight ahead with the knees slightly bent. The stomach is relaxed. When you have this posture correct it will feel as if you can draw energy up from the ground.

Head and spine. Hold your head as if it is suspended by a string attached to the crown. Make sure you do not tilt the head. Keep your lower and upper spine straight. The neck is aligned with the spine, allowing energy to flow along the spine through to the head. If you are not sure whether you are keeping the spine straight, tilt the pelvis forward very slightly and tuck your tail in. Tuck the chin in very slightly and you will straighten the back of the neck as long as you don't tilt the head forwards.

Upper torso. Relax the shoulder muscles so that the shoulders drop down. This relaxes the chest, allowing the breath to flow freely so that the energy can circulate freely.

Arms. Hold your arms in a relaxed position at the height of the navel. Keep elbows slightly bent. Let your arms face each other as if you are holding a large ball between the hands. If this is not a comfortable position for you, you may also hold the hands at chest level or move between the two positions, holding each for a few minutes. The Aether energy flows between the fingertips and palms. Internal energy moves outwards between the two hands.

Eyes. Keep your eyes relaxed and open with a soft focus. Let go of any tension in the eye muscles and let them softly focus into the distance. The best way to do this is to look out of a window if you are inside, or practise this outside where you can avoid focusing on a close object.

Face. Keep your mouth closed and relaxed and let your teeth lightly touch. If saliva collects, simply swallow it.

The breath. As you inhale, feel the lower abdomen expand. As you exhale it contracts. This is relaxed and natural. You don't need to force this at all. Follow the breath. Be aware of it rather than "do" it.

One way to stay in an altered state while being aware of how long you have been breathing for is to count your breaths. Simply count each time you exhale. Start with around fifty or sixty breaths, and expand the number over time.

As you breathe, you don't need to think about anything in particular. Notice whatever you notice. Notice without judgment. You may simply think about what is happening in your body, you may have thoughts about your daily life, or something more profound. It doesn't matter. Let the thoughts just drift though as if they were flowing past on a river. Just bring your mind back to the posture and the moment of now, either by counting exhalations or by telling yourself, "Now I am breathing."

Finish

At the end of the session, let your arms float down to the side of your body and let your hands relax there. Finish by rocking your body very gently, so you shake out the posture. Rock from side to side, letting the arms sway right to left and back again. Then circle round clockwise and then counter clockwise as if you are massaging your whole body in the Aether around you. Finish by relaxing your arms down by the side again. You are ready for the rest of your day.

The Moon Breath (Pranayama)

According to most ancient systems, including the hermetic system of Western magic and the Tantric traditions, the body and energy channels have right and left currents equating to masculine and feminine aspects of the energy. The right side of the body is masculine in nature. The right side helps work and concentration. The left side is feminine in nature and aids in such activities as rest, sleep and relaxation.

Alternate nostril breathing, known to the members of the Western Golden Dawn tradition as the "Moon Breath," helps you to achieve a balance in the right and left currents of energy in the body. According to Tantric thinking, breath control exercises, or pranayama, help you to attain a balanced meditative state. Without this we tend to have one side of the body and one type of energy more dominant than the other.

It is said in this tradition that people who practice pranayama can live for two hundred years. Whether or not that is true, this exercise has been used by Western occultists for many years as a way of increasing energy mastery.

As with the other breath exercises you will have practiced so far, this exercise involves deep breathing and helps you to learn to focus and cut out unnecessary distractions from the mind.

As you exhale, it may help your focus simply to say within your mind, "breath is flowing out now." When you inhale, quietly say within your mind "breath is flowing in now." Or you can visualise the Aether symbol. Notice the colour in which it appears to you. This may vary according to your need to bring different vibrations into your system, as each colour brings different energies to heal you depending on the needs of your Aetheric body.

THE METHOD

Sit with your spine straight to allow a clear channel of energy through the crown chakra.

Rest your right hand on your face. Touch the first and second fingers together and lightly touch the other two fingers on the left nostril with the thumb on the right nostril. Breathe in.

Close up the right nostril using the thumb, and exhale using the left nostril. Let the exhale be slow and relaxed.

Now breathe in the same nostril for half the time of the exhalation.

Now let the thumb relax and close the left nostril with the fingers. Repeat the inhalation and exhalation with the right nostril.

Continue breathing through alternate nostrils in a relaxed way for about five minutes or so. You will find over time you can make your exhalations longer – up to about twenty seconds or more. At first you may not be able to do this exercise for more than a few minutes, but regular practitioners have managed to do this breathing for an hour or more, so do persist with your practice.

Gaining this level of control over the breath will have physical effects on the body, changes to your brain chemistry and a deep connection with the energy in your body. However, be cautious and ask advice if you have a respiratory disease, as it can be bad for you in this case, so check with a doctor if this is so.

According to Tantric tradition, advanced practitioners of this can master the art of levitation and a deep connection to the higher levels of consciousness, giving rise to other mystical and spiritual sensations.

Third Eye opening meditation

By meditating you raise your vibration, allowing lighter energy to illuminate the darker energy of your unconscious, bringing into your mind realizations about your life. As you do this you open your third eye – the energetic point that allows you to link in to your psychic sense.

First, find a comfortable place to sit and relax. Sit up straight. When you do this for the first time make sure that you pull the curtains or make the room darker in some way.

Breathe comfortably so that your breathing relaxes.

Now focus on the third eye in a relaxed manner. Begin to notice the point of light. Let it come to you naturally so that you can welcome it to you in a totally relaxed way.

Then let go as you continue to notice the light.

This technique will expand your consciousness and awareness. Once you have done it a few times, your unconscious will find it much easier to do it as a matter of habit. It frees up the link with the Higher Self and again lays the ground work for more advanced techniques. You may notice your ability to see thought forms or other psychic phenomena grows after practicing this for a while, especially if you have prepared the ground by carrying out the other mastery techniques.

PSYCHIC METHODS
Telepathy

It is a very simple process but will take practice. Whenever you want to link with another person to tune in to their energetic field, all you have to do is to visualize the chords that connect you and see through your third eye the flow of Aether clear of any obstacles.

You can practice this with the permission of people you know, to hone your powers.

The process

Still yourself. You can use your breath to achieve Alpha State.

If the person you wish to link with is not present, then ask permission via your Higher Self. The words you can use are:

"I ask that this only be with permission and to the highest good of all concerned."

Now see chords coming from your third eye to the third eye of the person you want to tune into.

Close your eyes and connect in to the other person's energy field.

As you connect in, you will feel the flow of Aether either through a change of temperature or through a tingling or other sensation.

Notice what images come to you. Your Higher Self may give you words, pictures or other types of images.

You can also link with any THING or ANIMAL or PLANT on the planet. Practice tuning into objects and nature. Your powers to detect different vibrations and receive messages from the invisible universe will be heightened the more you open up your powerhouse mind.

LIFE PURPOSE AND OTHER GUIDANCE FROM THE HIGHER SELF

Active dreaming is a method you can use when you need to receive wisdom from your Higher Self. Your Higher Self has access to all knowledge, past, present and future, because it is the part of you that is not bound by the rules of time and space. It is the part of you that is available at any time and in any situation.

You can ask for general guidance, messages about future events or any question regarding life purpose or your general spiritual progress.

THE METHOD

Sit or stand quietly and breathe deeply.

Still your mind down to the alpha state. Now you are going to use the Ha Breathing method to raise your vibration further.

Ask your unconscious mind to open up the channels to the Higher Self so that you can receive the wisdom you need clearly.

Ha breathe for at least twenty minutes.

You will feel your whole body begin to tingle as it is filled with the higher vibrations of Aether.

As this happens you will feel your whole energy system open, and in particular your crown chakra on top of your head, as this is the connection point to the Higher Self energetically.

Open up your third eye. Do this simply by looking upwards between your eyebrows with your eyes closed, and noticing the light point. Or if you are sensitive you won't even need to do that, you will just be aware of the energy changing as your third eye opens.

Now become aware of an energy or aka chord extending from

your third eye to your crown chakra, connecting to the energy of the Higher Self and through your Higher Self to the boundless wisdom of the greater Spirit universe. As you continue to ha breathe, this connection is cleared of energy blocks to form a clean channel. You are connecting in through your psychic channel to this highest wisdom.

Stop breathing and be still. Ask your Higher Self any question that you need answering. Be observant. You may receive the answer clairaudiently (in the form of sound) or clairvoyantly (in the form of an image).

Once you have received the answer, then bring your energy chords back into your body and still yourself. When you are ready, open your eyes and write down the answer you received.

If the answer is symbolic, then ask yourself these questions:

What do I feel about this?

What does this say to me?

What do I see when I look at this?

Use your senses to guide you. Your feelings will often be the strongest indication as to meaning. With practice you will start to recognize the habitual ways in which your Higher Self likes to communicate to you. If you don't find it easy to interpret messages you receive, then ask your Higher Self to guide you further. It may do this by sending your more messages in your waking or sleeping dreams.

Synchronicity

The other way the Higher Self sends us messages is by synchronicity. As you go about your daily life, you suddenly encounter coincidences or messages in the environment that guide you to the meaning your Higher Self is trying to get across to you.

For example, suppose you ask your Higher Self what career choice you should make. You are wondering whether or not to study medicine or become a lawyer. Strangely enough, whenever you look at the TV it seems to be showing programmes on doctors. You don't get the message? Then you walk down the street and there is a billboard that says – "Why not retrain as a doctor?" Or you come across a minor accident in the street and see a man who has collapsed being helped by a doctor. All synchronicities are not as obvious as this, but some really are.

Finally

When I asked what I needed to write about a year ago in my active dreaming state I couldn't interpret the image I was given. I asked for guidance but still no answers.

Then two things happened. I walked along my local street where I have lived for over ten years. I suddenly noticed a side street I sometimes walk down as a short cut had a small name plaque on it. Why I had never noticed this before, I have no idea. It was called Angel Walk. "Well," I thought, "I am definitely getting nearer."

Then I got home and settled in for the evening. As I put my things away I saw a bag I had been given as a gift. On it was written "Why can't I have everything?"

So I decided to find out the answer.

CAN YOU HAVE EVERYTHING YOU WANT?

I hope that you find all the answers you are looking for through beginning these practices.

You will discover for yourself more techniques and tools that you can add into this basic structure I am sure. I hope that you find that you can have everything you want in your life that is to your highest good.

Lightning Source UK Ltd.
Milton Keynes UK
UKOW05f0144311213

223798UK00001B/33/P

9 781612 042183